Gringos
Traveling South of the Rio Grande

Other books by Phil Karber

Vagabond Memoirs

Postmarks from a Political Traveler

Fear and Faith in Paradise:
Exploring Conflict and Religion in the Middle East

The Indochina Chronicles:
Travels in Laos, Cambodia and Vietnam

Yak Pizza to Go:
Travels in an Age of Vanishing Cultures and Extinctions

Gringos Traveling South of the Rio Grande

Phil Karber

COTTAGE STREET PRESS

Cottage Street Press
Fayetteville, Arkansas
cottagestreetpress@gmail.com

ISBN: 979-8-234-00288-4

Front cover photograph by Phil Karber of Diego Rivera's monumental "History of Mexico" mural in the Palacio Nacional in Mexico City.

Introduction photo of Phil Karber and Jerry Whitlock in Lviv, Ukraine taken in 2017 by a bystander.

Back cover photo: Phil Karber taken by Joellen Lambiotte

Book and cover design: H.K. Stewart

Printed in the United States of America

For all Latin Americans *who suffered gravely
or made the ultimate sacrifice in their struggle
for Independence from colonialism*

Contents

I spent 33 years and 4 months in active military service and during that period I spent most of my time being a high-class muscle man for Big Business, for Wall Street and the bankers. In short, I was a racketeer, a gangster for capitalism.... I helped in the raping of half-a-dozen Central American republics for the benefit of Wall Street. I helped purify Nicaragua ...

— Major General Smedley Butler
Former Commandant, US Marine Corps, 1935

The author, Phil Karber, and fellow traveler, Jerry Whitlock.

Introduction

IN THE EARLY AUGHT YEARS I "imagined" penning a travel book that checkerboarded the planet, exploring the ways faith, politics and poverty defined cultures. Worldwide anti-Americanism was on the upswing, its latest iteration triggered by the "Coalition of the Willing" the United States mustered to invade Iraq on a hunch that Saddam Hussein had an active WMD (Weapons of Mass Destruction) program. He did not. The program ended after the Gulf War in 1991.

As only an obsessed peripatetic would do, at the time of the Iraq invasion I set off from where I was living in Hanoi to zigzag the globe, making several trips to the Middle East, North Africa, and North Korea. In 2005, my wife, Joellen Lambiotte, and I repatriated to the United States, but I still couldn't shake that bad case of itchy feet. Craving novelty, off I'd go to bus through Mexico and Central America or walk the streets of war-torn Kabul, Afghanistan, or train from Winnipeg to Churchill to see the world's largest congregation of polar bears. Home was a stopover, long enough to send my passport to D.C. or a local consulate in Boston for more visas, and then off again. After I had inked big chunks of the ambitious travelogue, I realized that I needed to divide it into more than one book. So, I did.

In 2012, Rowman & Littlefield published *Fear and Faith in Paradise, Exploring Conflict and Religion in the Middle East*. In 2015, more of the working manuscript made it into *Postmarks from a Political Traveler*, a compilation of travel essays, published by Paradigm (now Routledge).

After *Postmarks*, I hunkered down for several years, plucking a few pearls from the old text and worked on a coming of age travel book, *Vagabond Memoirs*, published in 2024 by Cottage Street Press.

Following *Vagabond*, I thumbed the pages of my Nat Geo World Atlas for what came next, and decided to circle back to the unpublished material of a bus trip down the Pan American Highway, through Mexico and Central America. Though eighteen years had passed since that memorable journey, the underlying themes—faith, politics, Indigenous poverty, anti-Americanism—struck me to be as relevant today as they were in 2007. The Spanish Conquest, inspired by 'gold, glory, and God,' the 1823 enactment of the Monroe Doctrine, and the 20th century American hegemony, are now embedded like atavistic memories in every jungle village and urban slum in the region.

"President William McKinley's self-described divine intervention in the Cuban war of independence against Spain in 1898 initiated the first era of twentieth-century anti-Americanism," wrote Julia Sweig in *Friendly Fire*. "Whether they invoked God, democracy, money, the protection of U.S. citizens, or the threat posed by outside powers, Teddy Roosevelt, William Taft, and Woodrow Wilson continued the southward expression of U.S. power with a total of twenty-eight interventions in Honduras, the Dominican Republic, Nicaragua, Panama, Mexico, Haiti, Costa Rica, and Guatemala between 1900 and 1921. Among other effects, these events served as demonstrations of American muscle for consumption by European powers."

By the time Franklin Roosevelt introduced the "Good Neighbor Policy," populist movements in Latin America had become synonymous with anti-Americanism. And when John Kennedy launched his Alliance for Progress three decades later, it was dead on arrival once the Bay of Pigs fiasco went down. Against this background, upon my arrival in 2007, the colonial hangover was pervasive and pounding like a bass drum.

Clock forward, in January of 2025, the 47th president of the United States, Donald J. Trump, deepened the divide, unleashing a whiplash-inducing torrent of senseless slights and provocations to our neighbors. To name a few, threatening to annex Mexico, Panama, Greenland, and Canada, renaming the Gulf of Mexico, waging a senseless war against Venezuela, pardoning Honduran drug kingpin Juan Orlando Hernandez, and imposing hyper-inflationary tariffs on our friends and neighbors, Mexico and Canada, who happen to be our two biggest trading partners. If anti-Americanism was stitched into the cultural fabric of our southern neighbors when I penned this manuscript, well, buckle up.

My own transcontinental rambles have taught me to follow the tug of curiosity, to listen and size up the burdens and dreams that perfect strangers carry with them, and to return home with the news of what I have witnessed. The best sermons are lived, they say, not preached: Experience, reflect, distill. So, come join me busing down an eye-opening stretch of rural roads collectively known as the Pan American Highway.

Pancho Villa, Frida Kahlo and Diego Rivera

Chapter One

IN THE WHITE GLARE of late winter's noon, I-35 was a languid procession of tractor-trailers. As we approached the border town of Laredo, Texas, the traffic drew to a standstill. Flowing the opposite direction was a steady stream of the 6,000-force convoy of fully loaded trucks that churn northward every day, headed for distribution centers, supermarkets, and factories in the heartland. Hitching on to this unending train of commerce are the drug cartels and destitute migrants, both drawn like gravity to the economic opportunities of America, or as they mockingly say in Mexico, *Gringolandia*.

Southerly, the direction my friend Jerry Whitlock and I were traveling, 350 billion dollars-worth of American goods crosses into Mexico each year. And since Mexico has highly restrictive firearm laws, the contraband cargoes piggybacking those exports are American-made assault rifles, armor-piercing pistols, and fragmentation grenades, often destined for the Mexican drug cartels.

In the U.S. there are over 80,000 federally regulated gun dealers, more than the combined franchises of Starbucks, Subway, McDonald's and Dunkin Donuts. On any given day those merchants barter and sell tens of thousands of the 400 million firearms owned by Americans, accounting for over a third of the world's known arsenal. It's the eloquence of those numbers that bedevil law enforcement agencies, along with journalists, politicians, random citizens, and Mexican and American soldiers on both sides of this border, all of whom are frequently caught in the crossfire of the drug cartels' turf wars. That they are shooting us with our own guns does nothing to shake the uniquely American faith in the broad powers of the Second Amendment right to "keep and bear arms." Or, inferentially, the American hunter's prerogative to use an assault rifle to knock down a duck. Gun control, they mockingly say, is hitting what you shoot at!

✪ ✪ ✪

The non-English-speaking taxi driver we had hailed from a local bus station peeled off I-35's last exit. He then wove through the narrow back streets of old Laredo before drawing up next to San Augustin Catholic Cathedral, a monument (I thought) to conquistador Don Hernando Cortes and New Spain, and to the public consciousness and deep devotion that shapes most daily lives from Laredo to Tierra del Fuego. The further south I traveled, the Latin peasants' piety—fasting, festivals of Lent, pilgrimages, alms-giving, exhaustive prayer and church-going—came to remind me more of the all-consuming zeal of Middle Eastern Islam. On this Sunday, poor and pious-eyed Hispanic Catholics flowed down the cathedral steps with bevies of kids in tow.

There on the banks of the Rio Grande, I shouldered my duffel bag while my good friend and fellow traveler rolled and steer-wrestled his airport-worthy luggage up and down steps (I couldn't convince him to go backpacker-style…yet). The plan was there was no plan, only the intent and time to hop buses to Panama for the next two months.

✪ ✪ ✪

Jerry, a former award-winning rodeo cowboy, was riding high as the founder/chairman of the largest non-carbonated drink packaging company in North America. Other than the Western hats he dons when in the sun's glare, he could be mistaken for a fiddle-footed metro-sexual. He wears a Billy Idol platinum haircut, designer sunglasses, and self-designed bell bottom jeans, attracting rock-star-grade attention. Plain spoken as his laid-back riffs on the glories of a fried bologna sandwich or the intricacies of dancing the Cotton Eyed Joe, he is gifted with an artist's eye, and when his mind's cracking, a cerebral cortex like a steel trap.

We met in North Korea in 2002, both of us there on black market visas, and came of age only eighty miles apart, he in Eastern Oklahoma and I in Northwest Arkansas, separated in age by three weeks. Since that two-headed-cow-of-a-tourist venture in North Korea, travel to unfamiliar places has drawn us together on several play-it-by-ear journeys. Obsessive wanderers, we both revel in jumping out of our skin and finding things we're not looking for, the improvised road trip and its many surprises on the fly that fork and fuse like an epic novel. Austrian poet Rainer Maria Rilke put it another way: "Let everything happen to you: beauty and terror. Just keep going. No feeling is final."

Companionable as we are, the lessons of the road that we take away—a widened perspective, reversing stereotypes—can be worlds apart. At the core of Jerry's self-identity, he is a roper and a wrangler. I call him Cowboy.

✿ ✿ ✿

In short order, we fell into the flow of an onslaught of swarthy Hispanics under a banner that said, "Gateway to the Americas." I did a double-take to assure myself that we weren't going the wrong way.

A fifty-cent ticket was required to pass through a turnstile that gave way to a footbridge on an aging iron railroad trestle over the Rio Grande River. Three other bridges of concrete and galvanized steel stretched alongside the footbridge, one to the north, two immediately south. In a pearly heat haze, car, truck and pedestrian traffic moved in both directions over the spans of this international divide, making it seem more crossroads than border frontier. From opportunity-seeking immigrants to Mexico's leaders, there is a pervasive and historical attitude here that says Mexico does not end at the Rio

Grande (especially with over sixty-five billion dollars in annual re-mittances from Mexicans in the U.S.). In villages around Mexico when the question comes up about where all the working-age men have gone, the answer is not America, but *"el norte."* Below the trestle, a well-kept park sprawled along the sunbaked banks of the mythical river, a sluggish ribbon of pea soup.

On the Mexico side of the river, a snarl of chubby customs officials, grinning like Cheshires, lingered in the shade by a green light for pedestrians. Which, had it turned red, would have been the signal for us to stop. Or maybe not. To locals the border towns are their neighborhoods, like different parts of the same city, sister cities linked by trade, by family and by religion, and the customs officials, especially those who are approached by cartel thugs, are known for ignoring the light. *"Plata* or *plomo,"* they say, which means "money or lead?"

On this day, no one asked for our *papeles* (identity papers). Our heads on a swivel, Cowboy and I treaded on until we melded into the bustling streets of Nuevo Laredo. We had nothing to hide, but the outlaws, scofflaws, drug runners and arms smugglers, those who have transported in over ninety-nine percent of the weapons that are now in the hands of Mexican criminals, might. If in their shoes, it would make sense to choose the route of our footsteps.

Bus touts, taxi drivers, and moneychangers assaulted us in front of *Farmacia el Puente,* barking and clapping like a pod of seals. A fold-ing A-frame billboard straddled the sidewalk, advertising Ampicillin, Viagra, Prozac, Valium and pain pills. But cheap pharmaceuticals were not on our minds. Pausing a moment, as sweat beaded on our fore-heads, we grabbed a small yellow taxi, stuffing ourselves into its snug telephone-booth confines before scudding through sulfurous clouds of exhaust fumes. As the tattered old trading town rolled by it seemed much had been modernized, yet old habits were dying hard. Within ten minutes, we had arrived at the Tica bus station.

After a haggle with the taxi driver, we pushed through a line of hawkers and haggard misfits and strode into the commotion of the departure lounge, a cacophony of gate calls, wheezing engines and trilling accents. We were catching an overnight bus.

Nuevo Laredo was famous in my post-army, college years for its tequila, drugs, prostitutes and unspeakable donkey shows, best consumed in that order. It was a more civilized era then, when switchblades and syphilis were the spoilers, not AIDS and AKs like today. But then and now, these border towns represent the least common denominator of humanity—exploitation of human misery—from Tijuana to Thailand. For those friends and fellow students who chose a walk on the wild side in Nuevo Laredo, on the fun-to-rowdy-scale there was an alluring, target rich accessibility here that spring break in Daytona Beach could not match.

❂ ❂ ❂

Today everything you read says the drug cartels have transformed Nuevo Laredo into the deadliest city of its size in North America. The favorite cantinas and cathouses are now boarded up; strait-laced tourists and day-tripping conventioneers arriving here for the cheap textile and leather goods have vanished.

In 2005, Alejandro Dominguez, the newly-elected police chief of Nuevo Laredo, who won a mandate to fight corruption, was murdered only hours after taking office. He was shot more than fifty times, as gruesomely executed as an ancient Aztec sacrifice. In 2006, turf battles between the Sinaloa and Gulf cartels, who employ psychotic Central American death squads to terrorize, left Nuevo Laredo with over 200 unsolved homicides, an average of one every forty hours. The current year was on course to exceed all others.

Days before our arrival, a congressman was wounded and his driver was killed. Throughout Mexico, over a two-year period, 5,000 politicians, police and innocent civilians were gunned down by drug cartels, more than Americans killed in Iraq in five years of fighting. Poverty aside, fueling this frenzy of homicides are weapons smuggled from the U.S., and the 200-billion-dollar annual demand in America for illegal drugs, especially cocaine and heroin, in many cases laced with fentanyl.

○ ○ ○

That spring break was over a long time ago for me and Cowboy was just another reason to push on. "Where you go?" said the long, slender, snake-eyed baggage handler in the departure lounge.

"Mexico City."

"Too big for me. They rob you in the daytime there." He stage-laughed, as if he were not also an easy target in this charnel theater of drug cartels.

Snake-eyes led us to a Mercedes bus that was seething with life. Dark-skinned men in white straw hats and women in blue *rebozos*, all warm and welcoming, hefted and wedged their boxes and bags and bundles into the overhead storage bins, and when those overflowed, the space beneath the seats was taken over. Insistently, the aroma of corn tortillas and musk of human flesh, crushed together like a pot of peas and carrots, wafted in the cool blown air.

As bus travel goes, for $25, we were riding high in the saddle, luxury class—soft reclining seats, a modular toilet, DVD screens, complimentary bottled water and cold food packs. Across the aisle, Cowboy and I shared beef jerky and salty peanuts. Soon Cowboy strapped on a neck pillow and tucked in for the night, as if in business class on a transoceanic flight.

Yet on the bus we were all the same, suspended animation on a nocturnal wander for the duration, sharing space with unknown faces, from unfamiliar places, all of uncertain means and motive. We had checked out of the mainstream and into life's rootless nitty-gritty. For me, there was a subdued apprehension about the mystery ahead, piquing the senses not into alarm, but with a keen alertness.

Between the harsh sounds of crashing gears and screeching airbrakes, we turned in the direction of the arid southwest, Monterrey and beyond, where the stark beauty of mesquite, organ cactus and maguey flourish in the way oak, maple and hickory do to the north. It's a fiery land of red-hot chilies, gut-burning tequila, feverish mountains, sun-browned faces and blazing skies. Yes, here, life burns. It's also a state of mind that seduces and suppresses at once, that steeps the pores as an aloe does on a hot day.

Outside, darkness fell like a curtain as we rolled through the *maquiladora* zone, where factories that import tariff-free parts and equipment for assembly or manufacture are then exported tariff-free to the States. As worldwide competition increases, as United States consumers demand more for less, the decision to outsource is a matter of simple arithmetic: labor costs in Mexico are one-sixth of those in the U.S. After the advent of NAFTA, the North American Free Trade Agreement, in 1994 (and the United States-Mexico-Canada Agreement, USMCA, in 2020) these maquiladoras spread—with rampant resistance from Indigenes and other small farmers—beyond the fifty-mile free-trade zone along the border to every state in Mexico.

The bus driver switched on the movie *Lord of War*, starring Nicolas Cage as a gun runner. Everyone watched with rapt attention, relishing the glorified violence of the American action movie that struck me to be as bloody as their crucifixes and canonized martyrs. Cage delivered tag lines like "The first and most important rule of gun-running is never get shot with your own merchandise" or "where there's a will, there's a weapon."

✿ ✿ ✿

Between the ear-shattering action scenes, and beneath a star-sprinkled Mexican sky, I read about one of Mexico's most famous folklore heroes. Pancho Villa is arguably to Mexico what Osama bin Laden is to many Middle Eastern Muslims: a ruthless villain who attacked the United States and became an inspirational force for anti-Americanism.

Little is known of Villa's early life other than that he was born to sharecroppers as Doroteo Arango in the state of Durango. He didn't assume the name of Francisco (Pancho) Villa until becoming the leader of a bandit gang. As the *rurales*, or mounted police, closed in on him, he moved north to the less populated Chihuahua state. There, a young "Pancho Villa" built a reputation as a smart but a murderous cattle rustler and train robber. In the turn-of-the-century years approaching the revolution, he went straight, so to speak, working as a muleteer for an American mining company.

Banditry alone, however, was not uncommon during the dictatorship of Porfirio Diaz. Landlords were a select few and ruthless, and the *campesinos* were legion and restless. These peasants were little more than indentured slaves, with scant hope of shaking loose of the grinding poverty. So, in 1910, when the Mexican Revolution began, bandit leader Pancho Villa was ready-made to battle the federales.

By circumstances of fate he suddenly found himself in a position of respectability—Colonel, General, Commander of the *Division del Norte, ciudad* of the state of Chihuahua, a Robin Hood character, fighting for the poor. *"Tierra y Libertad"* (Land and Freedom) became the rally cry for peasants wishing to take over the hacienda land. If Chihuahua State was the vanguard of this people's revolution, Villa was its face.

Villa enjoyed many victories, notably the crucial battle of Ciudad Juarez. The resignation of Porfirio Diaz followed, which ended over three decades of brutal dictatorship. Even President Woodrow Wilson threw in his support for Villa's peasant-based revolutionary army, supplying them with weapons that American arms factories were churning out for France and Britain in the early years of World War I. To boot, General John "Black Jack" Pershing hosted Villa across the Rio Grande from Juarez at Ft. Bliss, Texas. That cross-border conviviality soon went to hell in a hand basket.

The train massacre of a dozen American miners and businessmen near Santa Isabel by General Pablo Lopez, Villa's ranking field commander, signaled a blind hatred for Americans not seen before in Villa and his troops. Villa blamed his disastrous defeat by Carranza government troops in the Sonoran campaign on Americans, who allowed his opponents U.S. border sanctuary. Others would say, however, that Villa's uncommonly violent nature and lack of discipline made him unequal to the leadership mantle of the Division del Norte. He was reputed to shoot prisoners and civilian witnesses until his fellow officers of the Army of Liberation had had enough. Villa's defense was that he killed only when attacked or betrayed. President Wilson thought differently, withdrawing arms shipments to Villa, who had reverted to type, a Mexican model for many modern-day American allies gone bad.

Had it all ended there, Mexico would have had one less iconic hero. But with Villa now operating more like a cornered beast than a commander, his raiding force of several hundred crossed the border to Columbus, New Mexico. As for motive, one story says he was there to provoke an American backlash against the Mexico City government. Another has it that Sam Ravel, who owned a hotel and a hardware store that sold guns, took Villa's money, declared him a common bandit, and never delivered the weapons.

When Villa's rogue army stole into Columbus in the early morning hours of March 9, 1916, they attacked the 13th U.S. Cavalry garrisoned at Camp Furlong. They then torched downtown buildings, including Sam Ravel's hotel, killing seventeen in all, mostly civilians. Following the bugler's call to retreat, in the melee that followed, Villa's raiding forces (*Villistas*) fell back across the border where over 100 were killed. Meanwhile, Sam Ravel was in El Paso seeing a dentist.

Anti-Mexican sentiment swept the U.S. over this unprovoked attack on American soil, the first since the War of 1812. Soon, Villa's former admirer, Black Jack Pershing, was dispatched to the Mexican state of Chihuahua. With two brigades, over 6,000 troops of cavalry, infantry and artillery, and an air squadron of eight planes, Black Jack's incursion into Mexico was romanticized as the "Punitive Expedition."

It was at this juncture that the beard-the-lion hagiography of Pancho Villa found traction. For ten months the formidable American army scoured the rugged Sierras in search of Villa and the tattered remains of his loyal and battle-hardened troops. But the American forces came up empty, threw in the towel, and retreated across the border. Villa taunted the withdrawing *yanquis*: "Pershing came in like an eagle and leaves now like a wet chicken." That the invasion even occurred was humiliating to Mexico, so when the word spread that the great General Black Jack Pershing failed to capture Villa and the Villistas, an anti-American hero was born.

Four years later, in 1920, Villa was granted amnesty by the new Marxist government of Mexico. He returned to his home state of Durango. There he enjoyed his retirement on a government pension, as a prosperous *hacendado*. But in 1923, near the town of Hidalgo del Parral, while cruising in his Dodge touring car, he and five others were ambushed and riddled with bullets by assassins, hired by old enemies. That he went out in a blaze, at age forty-five-years-old, only burnished his confronting-danger-head-on legend in Mexico and Latin America, where even in death, flamboyance counts. Given a decade of image rehabilitation, thanks partly to Hollywood admirers, Pancho Villa has assumed the celebrated status accorded historical figures here such as Ignacia Zaragoza or Benito Juarez.

❖ ❖ ❖

All around us dull yellow lights sparkled like fireflies in a fog. Sleep had been fitful, the bus air stale but cool. We were entering the valley of Mexico, the former Aztec heartland, the kingdom of Montezuma. It was 4:30 in the morning. For the next two hours we groaned and lurched through the *"cinturion de miseria,"* or "belt of misery." Encircling the eight-million inhabitants of the metropolis of Mexico City, fourteen million *peones*, descendants of the Villa-era

24

laborers and farm hands, live in shantytowns, put together with cardboard and scraps of tin. They are mostly without proper sanitation and water, scrabbling for life among trash heaps. As such, the dry-as-a-biscuit hillsides in this liminal zone resembled the habitat of mud daubers, a self-replicating one that spread its woeful seed in all directions. Turkey buzzards gyred above in the early morning sky. It was a new day.

We rolled out of the Tica bus at the north station, and though a dirty brown halo of pollution covered the city, at over 7,000 feet altitude, the thin, chilled outside air tasted fresh. The jarring racket of tailpipes, the signature cry of the scrap metal trucks, the calls of the tamale vendors, and the awakening mass of humanity with their televisions blaring at once was softened only by the amber-hued morning light, washing over the modest but brightly painted residences, the *pulquerias* with cracking plaster, and the flat-roofed *supermercados*, boldly slashed with graffiti-cum-murals.

Relying on maps and gestures more than our Spanish skills, Cowboy and I hailed a taxi, and were soon checking into a youth hostel off the *zocalo*, or *Plaza de la Constitución*, in Mexico City's historic district. Falling in behind us were three young Canadian girls, peas in a pod. Their fashion sense, with eyebrows, lips, septums and ears pierced, and one with purple hair streaked in green, seemed more statement than style—not least being their backpacks that were sewn in an autumn forest of maple leaves. I didn't take this to mean that these youngsters were flag-waving patriots; they didn't fit anyone's profile of that. Rather the flag patches were meant to say "don't confuse us with gringos."

In third-floor communal showers, I washed off the stench of a long bus ride, dressed on the fly and caught up with Cowboy. As if it were our first hot meal in weeks, at a sidewalk taqueria we wolfed down a plate of huevos rancheros and frijoles, served up like a dark moon on a sunny sky. From there, we blinked our way into the bright, busy plaza facing the sooty gray Metropolitan Cathedral.

25

The postcard simplicity of short-statured couples—skinny *hombres* and chubby *senoras* strollin'—belied the glossy porno images of tight-bodied tarts sold like newspapers on every corner. American and German tour groups, *pulque*-besotted idlers, beady-eyed cops and unlicensed, roving market ladies with a blanket peddling a few pieces of Aztec kitsch, cluttered the sidewalk. At the whimsical wave of a cop's hand or the toot of his whistle, the unlicensed market ladies would pack up their trinkets and set up around the corner. Food carts of tropical fruits and fried corn tortillas circled the cathedral corner, the cloying smell of grease and chilies rising in the air.

❂ ❂ ❂

Don Hernando Cortes, representing the Holy Roman Emperor King Charles V, arrived in Mexico in 1519 armed with the Treaty of Tordesillas. Brokered by Pope Alexander VI to settle New World claims between Portugal and Spain, the treaty 's arbitrary dividing line in the Atlantic Ocean shaped the colonization of the Americas.

The conquistadors, believers in a faith that says "Thou shall not kill," had only recently routed the Moors of Spain. In doing so they had invoked their war god *Santiago Matamoros*, St. James the Slayer of Muslims. Once in New Spain, or Mexico, they called forth a war god apropos to their new enemy: *Santiago Mata-indios*, or St. James the Indian Killer. Given time, the vanquished, imitating their conquerors, would also find a new war god.

The building of the Spanish baroque Metropolitan Cathedral began with Cortes, and went on for three centuries. It straddles the soft footings of Tenochtitlan, which, upon the arrival of Cortes and his 500 men, was the heartbeat of the sacred Aztec precinct, 250,000 souls strong, larger than any European city at the time except for Constantinople. The Spaniards' grab for gold and the gusto in which they imposed a new god, however, all but extinguished this imperial city of pre-Columbian, planet America. Replacing the Aztec sacrifices, Cortes and his Franciscan priests gave Mexico a beheaded

John the Baptist and a crucified Jesus. The carnage that fell in Cortes's wake would have made Mohammed and his crusading caliphs, seven centuries before, look like peaceniks: twenty-five million Mexican Indigenes were killed or died from disease in less than a century.

Now, with soaring neo-classic bell towers, the cathedral is fissured by earthquakes and sinking into the soft clay soil, drained of the lagoon that once lay beneath it (which may be karmic). Aztecs believed Tenochtitlan to be the center of the universe, the unique coordinate where a Mexican eagle landed on a cactus, and clutched a serpent in its beak. This imagery is now emblazoned on the Mexican flag, a symbol of resurgence and self-assertion flying above the cathedral.

Culture follows power: pomp and grandiosity are tenacious forces. The view from the cathedral's flag and bell towers probably reached the same height as the sacrificial platform atop the former Aztec pyramid temple. From there, conquistador Bernal Diaz, accompanied by Cortes and Montezuma, thought the panorama to be out of a dream:

> So, we stood looking about us, for that huge and cursed temple stood so high that from it one could see over everything very well, and we saw the three causeways which led into Mexico. ...And we saw that from every house of that great city and of all the other cities that were built in the water it was impossible to pass from house to house, except by drawbridges which were made of wood or in canoes; and we saw in those cities Cues [temples] and oratories like towers and fortresses and all gleaming white, and it was a wonderful thing to behold; then the houses with flat roofs, and on the causeways other small towers and oratories which were like fortresses.
>
> After having examined and considered all that we had seen we turned to look at the great market place and the crowds of people that were in it, some buying and others

selling, so that the murmur and hum of their voices and words that they used could be heard more than a league off. Some of the soldiers among us who had been in many parts of the world, in Constantinople, and all over Italy, and in Rome, said that so large a market place and so full of people, and so well regulated and arranged, they had never beheld before.

❂ ❂ ❂

Cowboy and I crossed the busy Spanish plaza, laid out with the volcanic stones of the former Aztec temple. High-rent avenues spun off the plaza like shiny spokes on a dusty retread, giving on to nineteenth century, fin-de-siecle storefronts and palaces, where the wealthy *peninsulares* once resided. The National Palace was the most imposing of all, located on the east end of the plaza. Built in the Spanish colonial motif on the Aztec heights, it stretched prison-like for over two football fields. Greeted by a gauntlet of gun-toting guards, we entered the Halls of Montezuma (or the National Palace). Its courtyard arcades, put up over the former Aztec leader's residence, came to life like another universe with the ambitious murals of Diego Rivera.

Upon entering the "Halls of Montezuma," my mind was running amok with two contrary currents of emotion, at first conjuring the American marine's proud hymn my father whistled and sang at home in the fifties ("From the Halls of Montezuma...," the song goes). He was always upbeat, full of vitality when letting go of those patriotic verses. After all, it was the black and white days of post-World War II euphoria. The good guys defeated the Nazis and Fascism. Then, being an American abroad, especially in Europe, must have conferred something special, if not the moral high ground. But the U.S. military invading Mexico a century before, as the marine hymn rhapsodizes, was arguably even less heroic than the 1980s American-led invasion of the tiny country of Grenada. It's a nice fiction though, if you're not Mexican and on the receiving end.

"Gringos think we are a de facto colony, that we owe them something," said a Mexican woman named Maria who joined us in the Halls of Montezuma after recognizing us from the hostel. "I have many gringo friends who, how should I say, patronize me. It's their problem. I just overlook it. You have to. It's in their DNA." She was on to something. We had longer discussions at the hostel on the contentious history.

After the 1521 conquest of the Aztec Empire, it was from the same high grounds as the Halls of Montezuma that Cortes ruled as viceroy. Three centuries later an American governor presided in the Halls at the close of the Mexican-American War. Once the Treaty of Guadalupe Hildalgo was signed in 1848, ceding to the U.S. Texas, California, Nevada, Arizona, New Mexico and Utah, the American military and governor vacated the halls. With that treaty, the nation of Mexico was divided in half.

During and after the war, back in America there was a vigorous debate over Polk's war against Mexico. Black Jack Pershing was beside himself, saying politics had prevented him from "eating the Mexicans raw." Southerners were in favor of the aggression, abolitionists saw it as a slaveholder's grab for territorial power. Illinois Congressman Abraham Lincoln opposed the war because it was preemptive, while Henry David Thoreau went to jail for his anti-war acts of civil disobedience. President Ulysses S. Grant, who as a young lieutenant helped overrun Mexico City, would write in his memoirs:

> Generally, the officers of the army were indifferent whether the annexation was consummated or not; but not so all of them. For myself, I was bitterly opposed to the measure, and to this day regard the war, which resulted, as one of the most unjust ever waged by a stronger against a weaker nation. It was an instance of a republic following the bad example of European monarchies, in not considering justice in their desire to acquire additional territory.

Many viewed the Mexican War as a grand training exercise for junior officers who would later hold command roles on both sides of the American Civil War—Grant, Lee, Davis, Sherman, Meade, Jackson, Longstreet, McClellan. Today the annexed territory represents almost twenty-five percent of the U.S. landmass. (It's noteworthy that the current Hispanic population in the U.S. is bumping twenty percent.) Though the conquests, the treaties and the Gadsden Purchase may never be undone, locals will always consider the lost territory a cultural, historical extension of old Mexico.

○ ○ ○

In the Halls of Montezuma, Diego Rivera's brilliant murals spread like Quetzalcoatl, the Aztec plumed serpent god, along balconies and up balustrades, rising to an aerie of stairwell arches in techno-colored vignettes. It's an exhaustive allegory in which the artist pits the powerful and powerless—imperialists and capitalists exploiting primitive socialism, a visual language that spoke vividly of revolution.

In the mural, Cortes, thought to be the second coming of Quetzalcoatl, clenches a spear and faces off with Cuauhetemoc, the last Aztec emperor, holding a sling. Above the rust-plumed eagle, with a tangerine-hued serpent in its beak, is Father Hidalgo, portrayed as leading Indian peasants to Independence from Spain. Once Napoleon I stripped Charles IV of the divine right to rule the Spanish empire, Hildalgo's revolution cascaded through Latin America.

Indians, Diego's noble savages in the murals, were dressed in white breech clothes and presented as lambs to slaughter by conquistadors with muskets and priests with Bibles. As with the Maya stele that once chronicled names and events, Zachary Taylor, Benito Juarez, Portfirio Diaz, Emiliano Zapata, Pancho Villa, took their place on these stone walls of storied legends.

While deeply woven with Diego's Marxist twist, the mural both mothers and mirrors modern Mexico's cultural paradoxes. Indians are eulogized, and have always been subjected to discrimination. The Spanish invasion, inquisition and destruction of Aztec culture are widely abhorred, but the blood of these evil-doers flows through seventy-five percent of Mexicans. Ninety percent of Mexico today, including the poor Indigenes, is Catholic. Yet the tension between church and state is always at a tipping point.

When Diego joined the Mexican muralists, the church was outlawed in Mexico, the disturbing theme of Graham Greene's novel *The Power and the Glory*. It was the time of the holy war—*la Cristiada*. In two and a half years more than 70,000 people were killed, including some ninety priests. Mexico did not resume formal diplomatic ties with the Vatican, the biggest landowner and richest institution in Mexico, until 1992. In the same vein that Jefferson described the tree of liberty, it takes some periodic blood in the streets to refresh the notion of separation of church and state.

❂ ❂ ❂

From the time of the Mexican-American War, Mexico has sought to limit U.S. power in Latin America. After the revolution, Frida Kahlo and Diego Rivera, together as artists, as husband and wife, and, for the most part, as avowed communists, came to represent an attitude of nativism, of anti-imperialism among Mexicans. In the late '20s, when Nicaraguan guerillas were fighting an occupation force of U.S. soldiers, the guerilla leader, General Augusto Sandino was granted asylum in Mexico. In the mid-1950s when Che Guevara and Fidel Castro needed a remote jungle to train their guerilla armies, Mexico, at that point a deep-dyed cauldron of revolutionary boldness, welcomed one and all. And during the '80s civil wars in El Salvador and Nicaragua, it was Mexico's petrodollars that supported the leftist forces against U.S. interests.

Undoubtedly, Mexico contributed twice as much to the Sandinistas as did the Soviet Union. From the early '20s through the late '40s, when prominent communists arrived in Mexico, as a matter of course, they were feted in Frida and Diego's home. Today, the renegade couple's influence in Mexico and Central America may be stronger than ever.

❂ ❂ ❂

Cowboy and I steered clear of the gathering crowds of tourists, escaping underground at the Zocalo/Tenochtitlan metro station. We were working our way to the suburb of Coyoacan, which in *Nahuatl*, the language of Aztec descendants, means "place of the coyotes."

Lean and grim-faced, Indian women and their children, all wrapped in varying-sizes of shabby *serapes*, sprawled like refugees on the subway steps. Hair matted with lice, mamas picked away with one hand while begging with the other. Cowboy did a double-take. "If you put them on a set of scales," he said, "a family of five wouldn't weigh 100 pounds."

Six miles southwest of the zocalo, Don Hernando Cortes encamped at Coyoacan after the fall of Tenochtitlan. More famously today, however, it is the neighborhood of the former Kahlo family home, now the Museo Casa Estudio Diego Rivera y Frida Kahlo. The leafy suburb, purpled with jacaranda, is trendy with restaurants and boutiques set among fountains and well-kept parks. The stucco homes are shaded in gay pastels, protected by high walls topped with coils of razor wire, and laden with history.

Russian revolutionary Leon Trotsky took up residence in Coyoacan in the mid-thirties, exiled and under orders of assassination from Joseph Stalin. In 1940, King Carol II of Romania fled here after being dethroned. The museum, painted a bold blue with wide red perimeter stripes, and long green shutters secured by iron grates, perches like an overgrown peacock on the corner of Londres and Allende streets.

❂ ❂ ❂

According to Frida biographer Hayden Herrera, Wilhelm Kahlo, of Romanian Jewish descent but born in Baden-Baden, Germany, immigrated to Mexico in 1891. Estranged from his father, who had remarried after his mother's death, he changed his name to Guillermo, and never returned to Germany. A steady flow of Europeans was sailing the Atlantic at the time: Dictator Porfirio Diaz, who set upon modernizing Mexico on the backs of the poor, sought the foreign capital of industrialists and commercial landowners. Guillermo and other rugged individualists fell in the wake. *Malinchismo*, the desire for anything foreign, a word coined from the name of Cortes's mistress, was a catchword at the time among the Mexican elite. Without money or capitalist guile, Guillermo Kahlo blended into this pre-revolution culture of Mexico.

Guillermo fathered two children in a first marriage, which ended tragically two years later with the sudden death of his wife. Soon afterward he courted and married Matilde Calderon, the daughter of an Indian father and Spanish mother, from the valley of Oaxaca, south of Mexico City. It was then that Guillermo enjoyed a fleeting moment of fame and prosperity as a photographer. He bought property and built the *Casa Azul* (Blue House), where Frida was born, came of age, and lived famously with husband Diego Rivera. After Diego paid off the mortgage on Casa Azul, Guillermo deeded the property over and moved three blocks away.

As a child, Frida contracted polio, leaving her with a withered right leg and foot. Making matters worse, in late adolescence she sustained a spinal and pelvic injury in a trolley crash. Given those incurable maladies, Frida suffered with a life of surgeries and pain, always nipping at the edges of her strength. Out of this anguish an artist was born, not as a Surrealist tapping into an abstract subconscious, as Andre Breton imagined, but as an interpreter, in colorful images, of the frightening episodes of her life, the physical agony she endured, portrayed as gruesomely as the Mexican churches depict the Passion of Christ on the road to Calvary.

Frida was a people's princess. She smoked like a chimney, told dirty jokes, always sported a silver flask of *mescal* and flaunted her *alegria*

33

the way a "peacock shows its." Ever accessible, Frida enjoyed a variety of men and women as lovers, including house guest and Rivera comrade, Leon Trotsky. For someone never far from pain, Frida viewed sex as "a way of enjoying life, a vital impulse." She was fond of glamour and money as a means, and noblesse oblige as an end, while also playing the heroic sufferer.

Frida had a love-hate relationship with America, despite doing a deep dive into the social whirl of New York and California for four years with Diego (and her other paramours). She and Diego were often feted at high-toned parties, venues to peddle their proletariat art to Yankee capitalists at dear prices. While milking one breast, goes the saying, Frida mauled the other, detesting the Americans' unbridled ambition, the need to be the *grande caca*, or big shit, a favorite expression of hers. I don't particularly like the gringo people," she wrote. "They are boring and they all have faces like unbaked rolls." It was even Frida who minted the mocking nickname for America, "Gringolandia." It's not clear, however, that she ever sought out the American hoi polloi, who would have been unacquainted with her silk stocking inner circle of Rockefellers and Firestones.

⊙ ⊙ ⊙

Regarded as the "Lenin of Mexico," Diego fell out with Stalin over Soviet totalitarianism. Trotsky, who championed a more decentralized, worldwide brand of communism, was, for the moment, ideologically simpatico with Diego. So, when Mexico granted Trotsky asylum after he was expelled from Norway, Frida was at the docks in Tampico to welcome his ship. Upon debarkation, Trotsky's wife Natalie expressed her apprehension about a Soviet-ordered assassination of her husband. Curtailed by a kidney condition, Diego wasn't at the docks but awaited them at the train station in Mexico City.

With upgraded security and bodyguards, Trotsky soon moved into the Casa Azul, then a lively venue for pre-Cold War political debate and anti-American rhetoric. Two years later, feelings began to change between Trotsky and Diego, who was unaware of Trotsky's affair with Frida. Their differences were more about temperament than ideology, Diego whimsical with a magpie mind, Trotsky a worried didactic.

Losing their welcome at Casa Azul, Trotsky and Natalie moved around the corner, where Natalie's worst fears played out. Trotsky was assassinated with an ice pick to the brain by a Soviet agent, who gained Trotsky's confidence by making known his friendship with Diego and Frida. The blustering, gun-toting Diego was a suspect, but was never charged. As memories dimmed, six years later Diego rejoined the Stalinist Mexican Communist party.

Diego was fascinated with American technology and its application to the coming revolution. His celebrated murals, "Detroit Industry," at the Detroit Institute of Arts, and "Man at Crossroads," created for the RCA Building at Rockefeller Center, plumbed his syncretic ideas of industry and revolution. The RCA mural was famously destroyed when Diego refused Nelson Rockefeller's demand to paint over Lenin's mug.

Brushing up with the American kahunas of capitalism was a tango Diego could dance. Driven by their adulation, by the healthy paychecks and by his ideas of pan-Americanism, after the Stalin-Hitler pact of 1939 Diego saw the U.S. as a partner in an anti-totalitarian solidarity movement. Following author Hayden Herrera's account, "his real political aim, he told Sigmund Firestone in a letter dated January 30, 1941, was to establish 'a common citizenship' for everybody in the Americas and to destroy the leading totalitarians of the era: Hitler, Mussolini, and Stalin. He wanted to create a single democratic intercontinental culture, a union, he said, of the ancient traditions of the South and the industrial activity of the North."

The tropical trees and desert flowers seemed like leftover props to the menagerie that once gathered in Casa Azul's colorful courtyard: Bonito the parrot who slept with Frida, its male counterpart who drank beer and tequila and cried on cue (I can't get over this hangover), the bald Aztec dogs, the tame doves, the domesticated deer, the caged chipmunks and the chirping osprey.

A tableaux of Judas masks adorned an open-air space beneath Frida's studio where her students, friends, family, fellow artists and activists once congregated. Frida collected these masks not so much as reminders of the betrayal of Christ, for she was an atheist, but instead as symbols of enemies of the people—such as landlords, soldiers, policemen and politicians.

Leading from the courtyard was Diego's room, where his noblesse oblige attire fell around his bed: scruffy, black leather miner boots, denim overalls, Stetson hat. Missing was his holster and gun, not an uncommon adornment in post-revolutionary Mexico. One of Frida's Tehuana dresses and a *rebozo* were displayed next to the kitchen, which, tiled in blue, white and yellow, and scattered in clay pots and drinking vessels, imitated the humble décor of the campesinos' mud homes.

Slants of broken light pierced the courtyard trees and the second story windows of Frida's studio. Today her palette and wheelchair bracket an unfinished portrait of Joseph Stalin, as if she were taking a break. Self-portraits, letters, books, toys, dolls, Diego's pre-Columbian clay pots, and papier mache heads became the studio medley easily viewed as fragments of her broken life. Often bedridden, especially so in her last years after the amputation of her right leg, she died in 1954, at age forty-seven.

Next to the studio we had a peek at her bedroom, dominated by a four-poster-bed with a canopy mirror, employed less to reflect her carnal liaisons than to paint self-portraits, famously highlighting her unibrow and dark, piercing stare, a narcissistic side effect of her bed-ridden years. Those years were also spent injecting thousands of vials of Demerol, morphine and other narcotics, to block her pain, and to some extent, reality. A plaster corset lay atop her bed, while her vintage wooden crutches rested nearby. A ghoulish figure hung from a poster like a fetish, there to sleep with, to keep the specter of death ever present.

A montage of Marx, Engels, Lenin, Stalin, and Mao portraits hung at the head of the bed, a spiritual family gathering. Only a few days before Frida died, from this bed she brushed the words *Viva la Vida* in crimson on her last completed painting, a vibrant still life of watermelons, now displayed in the downstairs museum.

Today, Frida's paintings fetch astronomical prices, much more than Diego's. "In Mexico, Kahlo's ubiquitous image, on everything from tote bags to tumblers, has become the counter-Guadalupe, complementing the numinous Virgin as a deathless icon of *mexicanidad* [pride in being Mexican]," reported *The New Yorker*. And since Frida and Diego have been safely dead for well over half a century, as a spruced-up love story, they have become national treasures, all but preserved in aspic. Marking the centennial of the Mexican Revolution, in 2010, Banco de Mexico, the country's Federal Reserve, announced that their faces and select paintings would grace opposite sides of the new 500-peso note.

That they were atheistic, Stalinist communists; that Frida's drug use would have given Jim Morrison pause; that Diego's abusive personality was matched only by Frida's hot-blooded, public rages; that their combined promiscuity would have made Andy Warhol's Factory crowd seem prudish, are collateral to the prism through which their doting countrymen view them: A love story of anti-American, populist artists.

❂ ❂ ❂

The morning after visiting Casa Azul, Eric Garcia, a light-skinned *mestizo* in his late twenties and a graduate student at the National Institute of Anthropology, introduced himself in a coffee shop around the corner from our hostel. He had learned his perfect spoken English while living with a family "Down Under," with only a hint of the Aussie accent. Eric had agreed to take us to the Basilica of Guadalupe, Mexico's holiest worship site, and from there to the ancient metropolis of Teotihuacan.

"We have a symbiotic relationship with the U.S.," Eric said after I questioned him over coffee about local attitudes. "Our cheap labor and your money bring us together, but there are cultural and historical conflicts." He added, in a rift of unveiled soap box rhetoric, "We [Mexicans] don't see the U.S. to be as powerful as they were. Iraq broke the American sword, and now from here to Argentina the euro is becoming as common as the dollar. The EU used Spain as the linchpin to develop and outsource to Latin America. We used to have only gringo cars here, but now we have Japanese, Korean and European."

Ever antsy, Cowboy popped up, saying, "Let's make like horse turds and hit the trail." We walked over to the metro, taking the blue line to Hidalgo station, where we changed trains onto Garrido, the stop nearest to the Basilica. Ten minutes later we fell in among the shopping legions at a massive market of hawker stalls selling religious CDs, ex-voto icons, candles, and Bibles. Cowboy called it Mexico's answer to "Bass Pro Shop."

"The Vatican has twenty-four million visitors a year, but ninety percent are tourists," Eric said. "The Basilica of Guadalupe has twenty million arrivals each year, but ninety percent are here for religious reasons." Eric continued as we beheld an ill-planned mountainside crammed with Moorish domes, encircled by a steady stream of pious peasants with ant-like purpose. Set alone, each church and altar evoked magic, as does a fine piece of art, but the higgledy-piggledy crush of it all was vulgar and uninspiring. It was a city unto itself, where the centerpiece, the old Basilica of Guadalupe, was tilted by earthquakes from left to right like a leaning Tower of Pisa. To its side was the new, low-slung Basilica—heavily anchored against the upheaving forces of frequent tectonic shifts. It was more reminiscent of a spherical tabernacle in Utah than one of Mexico's more common Baroque holy of holies.

"The revelation of the Virgin of Guadalupe is no different from Fatima in Portugal or Lourdes in France," Eric explained. "Mexico wanted its own Virgin."

❂ ❂ ❂

The Virgin of Guadalupe is a dark-skinned incarnation of the Virgin Mary. In 1531, only nine years after the conquest, as the story goes, she revealed herself to Aztec potter Juan Diego. Upon informing the Spanish bishop, the potter was directed to return to Tepeyac, the scene of the miracle, and bring back a sign. Once there, he again spoke to the Virgin, who told him to gather flowers, even though it was winter and they would not ordinarily be in bloom. As it happened Juan Diego soon came upon Spanish roses. When he presented them to the Franciscan bishop, they fell from his *tilma*, a poor-quality cactus cloth, whereupon an apparition of the Virgin was imprinted. That the miracle took place at Tepeyac, where Aztecs once worshiped *Tonantzin*, a moon goddess who on occasion doubled as mother goddess, gave the Indigenous spirits a link with the Christian god. The synthesis worked, a Christianized Tonantzin was born.

In the next decade, having lived in blissful ignorance of heaven and hell, like lemmings to the sea, over ten million Indians in Mexico became Christians. Churches sprang up like mushrooms after a tropical deluge, faster than at any time in any place in history. Clocking forward, the new Mama of Mexico was put to work: Father Hidalgo led the Independence movement with the rallying cry, "Death to the Spaniards and long live the Virgin of Guadalupe." A century later when Emilio Zapata's revolutionary army entered Mexico City, they waved Guadalupan banners. Like the Spanish war gods, Santiago Matamoros (St. James the Slayer of Muslims) and Santiago Mata-indios (St. James the Indian Killer)—or the more ecumenical Christian and Muslim war god, St. George—Mexico had found a guiding force.

Mexican novelist Carlos Fuentes stated matter-of-factly, "…one may no longer consider himself a Christian, but you cannot truly be considered a Mexican unless you believe in the Virgin of Guadalupe."

✪ ✪ ✪

This was an ordinary Wednesday, no religious holiday, yet thousands filed through the modernist church. Downshifting to a more sheep-like gravity, we fell onto a horizontal escalator, which glided beneath Juan Diego's tilma bearing the Virgin's apparition, ringed in an aureate glow. All the while, dark, pious eyes aloft, pilgrims crossed themselves and rubbed their rosaries while transiting the force field. From there, devotees queued in front of a semi-circle of at least fifty confessional booths, seeking forgiveness, invoking the Virgin's name, or interchangeably "Our Venerated Mother of Tonantzin," the Aztec goddess.

"They come to thank her for little or a lot because we don't have social security here," Eric whispered. "It is important to be thankful and to get forgiveness." Crowded as it was, Eric pulled me aside to add that for those who could afford the Internet, it was now acceptable to e-mail confessions.

We jumped the confession line bedlam for the short switchback up Tepeyac. Soon we were passing a towering bronze sculpture of Pope Juan Pablo (John Paul), dedicated in 1999 when he canonized the Aztec potter Juan Diego. The statue was monarchal, if not Crusader-like: The pope's ceremonial miter was the size of a five-gallon wash drum, his cassock lifted to the air as if Superman were taking off, while he brandished the enchanted scepter more like a hot iron to brand with than as a beacon of gentle Jesus. The decrepit Church of Guadalupe slanted unsurely over the statue, which Eric drew back from. "I don't go near there. It gives me the creeps with the earthquakes and sinking building," he said, as I walked inside, caught once again in the slipstream of prayerful peasants.

There were other reasons to get the heebie-jeebies here. Operatic hymns played, murals rose up the walls like curtains of cinematic splendor, the Virgin was central, with the eagle gripping the writhing snake (of the Mexican origin myth) next to her. The truly jarring images were the veristic statues of *Cristo Rey*—Christ the King—his body full of bloody, suppurating stigmata. This struck me more as a grisly Hollywood re-creation that Quentin Tarantino might have imagined than the iconic inspiration of a prayerful stopover to salvation. The churches in Mexico are chock-full of these macabre, real-life sculptures, the bloodier it seems the more powerful the supernatural power, or *mana*.

Mexicans don't mind getting up close and personal with death, Eric avowed: taunting it, playing with it, courting it, worshiping it, just as their pre-Hispanic ancestors had done. Among the Aztecs, for example, it was fortuitous to die in battle or by human sacrifice, a better spot in the afterlife was assured (so too in Islam). Today, Mexico's most celebrated holiday is *Dia de Muertos*, or Day of the Dead (also All Souls and Saints Day), at which time they return home to celebrate, to make graveside offerings to deceased friends and relatives, to adorn family altars with skeletons and ghoulish toys (not unlike ancient Egyptian and current Chinese traditions). Here, their pagan past often seeps into the Christian present and *vice versa*, where nothing is exactly what it seems: Did god create humans? Or did humans create god?

Outside and up the steps, a bronze donkey, Juan Diego's I supposed, stood in front of the Virgin, encircled with plastic roses—a sign of fertility. Like herding quail, tour guides led the better-heeled, selfie obsessed pilgrims with cameras or cellphones. As we reached the summit of Tepeyac, Mexico City unfolded beneath a burnt sienna ring of smog. While Indian families stepped around us, Eric said the pea-souper could be worse: in 1989 schools were closed for the month of January due to excessive particulate matter in the air.

"There are five million cars in this city of twenty-two million. Families of means have several, while the poor have none," Eric said.

"Over two million people here live on less than five pesos a day [$.75]. Only Sao Paulo, Brazil [largest Catholic country] has a wider gap between rich and poor." Eric bemoaned the population crisis, and reading between the lines, the church's role. He mused aloud that when the new Pope visits Guadalupe for the first time, that he will sanctify a goddess of Planned Parenthood. The auguries are not promising, I muttered.

❂ ❂ ❂

The Sun pyramid rose like a magic mountain from the Valley of Teotihuacan, the place where, they say, humans became gods. Maguey cactus abounded, commercially grown in this sun-bleached, sacred high valley. Its products of paper, needles, thread, soap, mescal and pulque, the milky low-alcohol brew known as the "champagne of peasants," was hawked along with obsidian carvings to all who arrived.

At the gate of the ancient city, Eric and a fellow guide jumped into a conversation, punctuating every sentence with gringo this or gringo that. Seeing me react with a sharp glance, he assured me it was not derogatory, yet he added, with a hint of rebuke, "We don't call you Americans because we are also Americans. We were here before you." Drill down to the core of any local's limbic system and my guess is you'll find a comparable default mode.

❂ ❂ ❂

Teotihuacan was settled circa 400 B.C., but the first architectural glories didn't go up until around the time of Christ. At its zenith, from the 1st through the 7th century, Teotihuacan was the largest city in pre-Columbian America, with up to 150,000 inhabitants. By comparison, Cahokia, a cluster of small farms near present-day St. Louis, without the grand pyramids and palaces, had only 20,000 residents in its 9th century heyday.

The *Piramide del Sol* (Pyramid of the Sun), was built in the 1st century, and but for Cheops, is grander than all other Egyptian pyramids. Human backs, corvee labor, handled the heavy lifting here.

Draught animals—horses, mules, oxen, donkeys or camels—did not exist at the time in this hemisphere. So, who were these Siberian migrants, these ancient builders? Apart from their shared attributes with the Olmecs, the mother culture, the Teotihuacans' identity remains lost in the mists of pre-Hispanic America.

Teotihuacans had a highly organized society, the 260-day calendar, and used the bar and dot system for writing. Otherwise, there was no Rosetta Stone left behind. We know nothing of their rulers, their chronological history, their language or even what they called this urban and religious Mecca. The name Teotihuacan, meaning Place of the Gods, was given by the Aztecs.

Teotihuacan likely wielded some degree of military and political control over a vast trade network, one that extended from the Maya cities of Guatemala to the Indian enclaves of Colorado. As a metropolis of industry there were jewelers, potters, and craftsmen, yet cultural development in first millennia Mexico was dependent on agriculture—therefore water and maize were holy. Quetzalcoatal, the Plumed Serpent, a symbol of fertility and regeneration, and also of the duality of spirit and matter, emerged at this time to become the most enduring cult of Mesoamerica.

In 1923, when author D.H. Lawrence stopped off here, he declared Teotihuacan greater than the ancient ruins of Rome and Pompeii. He reported that Quetzalcoatal was more alive at that time than the Spanish churches in Mexico. The Avenue of the Dead, which runs north and south, connecting the Sun and Moon pyramids with the Temple of Quetzalcoatal, was named by the Aztecs. The hundreds of apartments and palaces of the elite that rimmed the ancient promenade were thought to be tombs.

As such, to visualize Teotihuacan in the round at peak glory both humbled and captivated me, walking through history and imagining the lives and creative forces that came before us. The Sun and Moon pyramids plastered in crimson red among a shiny sea of red and white tips thrusting to the sky; sparkling rivulets cascading from the nearby mountains, funneling into aqueducts which veined the metropolis as a giant cooling system. Priest kings in feathered headdresses would have mounted the fire-topped pyramids in ceremonial splendor. Conch shells might have blown, while reed flutes whistled like a song-filled wind. Dogs and turkeys and kids, with wheels for toys, would have shared play space. While the laity would have ritually propitiated the gods, they would have also populated the cobblestone market, exchanging goods, maize and maguey from their fields, turquoise from Durango, bear skins from Arizona and New Mexico, jaguar heads, quetzal plumes and jade from Guatemala, gold from Oaxaca, obsidian from the valley of Mexico.

Eric decided to loop off into a shady spot after walking the Avenue of the Dead. I set out alone to begin the short climb up the Sun and Moon pyramids. Cowboy demurred, saying that he had been there and done that, and would see the top of those pyramids from an airplane before he'd ever climb them again. As I was parting, Cowboy asked Eric about sacrifices here, or as he put it, the ripping out of hearts with knives fashioned from the obsidian being sold by the hawkers.

"Warriors were sacrificed to the sun, women to the moon, and children to the rain," Eric responded in a defensive tone, as if pre-Columbian Mexico were his true blood, or his purest truth, and all else was an abstraction. He then said, "Remember the Inquisition? The Reformation? When Cortes arrived in Mexico, back in the public squares of Europe, there were more killed in the name of God than were here to appease the gods." He was on to something, but I could see from Cowboy's puzzled aspect that he thought that killing for Jesus might be more humane than a sacrifice for a bountiful crop of maize.

The Sun pyramid is over 200 feet high, as vertical as a fifteen-story building. Its steep-pitched stairways were guarded by feline tutelary heads. A family of well-nourished locals fell in behind me, while a seventy-plus-year-old German woman, checking her step, aided by a cane, descended with a smile on her face. As it happened, all of those returning from the top of a certain age appeared to be infused with the triumphal spirit of Rocky. While pausing halfway up for a quick gaze over my shoulder, a shrewish-looking British woman of my age stepped down beside me, pointed at my paunch, and hee-hawed. Another, a sprightly Scandinavian woman, halted, and said, "Keep going, you can make it."

"Fuck you, wimps," I said beneath my breath. "I've run three marathons."

Frankly, fresh into town, standing in the withering sun at over 7,600 feet, it's possible that I came off as red-faced and breathless. To dispel such notions, I vaulted on up, two steps at a time. On top, 248 steps below me, my heart racing like a hamster, sucking up the pyramid power were two Aussie women sunbathing in bikini tops and jean shorts. An Indian man in a poncho and ponytail sat away, Buddha-style, and played a Simon and Garfunkel cover on a reed flute (I'd rather be a hammer than a nail...). A hot wind blew. One of the sunbathers sat up briefly from her sun-struck meditation to inform us that provincial Teotihuacan was more spellbinding than the Pyramids of Giza, pointing out that they are now encroached on by the urban clamor of Cairo.

The sunbather was on to something, as was early 19th century explorer and writer John L. Stephens, who had a few weighty thoughts to add:

> ...I have a conclusion far more interesting and wonderful than that of connecting the builders of these cities with the Egyptians or any other people. It is the spectacle of a people skilled in architecture, sculpture, and drawing, and [other] arts not derived from the Old World, but originating and growing up here, without models or masters, having a distinct, separate, independent existence: like the plants and fruits of the soil, indigenous.

❂ ❂ ❂

Below, the stone-wall outlines of the former metropolis spread to the purple-fruited nopal cactus farms, to the emptiness of desert scrub and cactus. Beyond were low-slung villages, draped in the glass banners that are strung up for Mexico's many religious festivals. At its zenith Teotihuacan covered eleven square miles, all the way to the smoky gray Sierra Madres, the ancient city's water source for 700 years. Given the rain and fertility gods, its alignment with the cardinal points, its vital astronomical force seemed hard to deny. Its collapse came on relatively fast: drought, famine, the chaotic warring that accompanies such catastrophe, perhaps. Whether real or imagined, astral architecture such as this, by, if nothing else, its sheer immensity, evokes a fascination that is magnificently holy.

Back along the Avenue of the Dead, plump, dusky-faced peddlers of schlock plopped in the shade of former palaces. Like startled birds issuing a rising pitch of warning calls, they whistled and sounded at each passerby, eagle-eying for a cue to pursue. Their sluggishness, however, reminded me more of sated geckos than spry avians. In the 1930s Aldous Huxley traveled here and characterized Mexican crafts as the "ghosts of good artists dictating to bad artists." On this day the obsidian carved masks, the brightly painted *tortugas*, the frilly pink and green bows and arrows, and the tequila bottles adorned with the faces of Aztec deities, were the updated version of the poor derivative art Huxley chronicled. They were nice souvenirs for a college dorm room, selling like hot tortillas to unfulfilled tourists of all types.

After the short climb up the Moon pyramid, I found Cowboy spread beneath the dreamy bower of a lone Pirul, a tree that droops like a willow and has a peppery scent. Nearby, an old model, paint-chipped Volkswagen slotted in next to a perfectly painted yellow American school bus. On the opposite side of the bus, a mid-sixties-model red Valiant drove up. The driver's head dithered like a bumble-bee, but barely rose above the chromasaur's steering wheel. A fuzzy-faced thirty-something man in a yellow do-rag emerged to remove from the passenger window a screwdriver, which he used to jerry-rig the glass and keep it in place. For security, he tugged the window up and jammed the screwdriver back into the door cavity. He then locked the door. After untying the trunk, he strained to lift a stack of what looked like the largest straw sombreros ever braided.

The sight of it all brought Cowboy to his feet. He wanted a brimmed hat for the blazing sun, plus he is rabidly acquisitive. We had seven weeks of buses to ride between here and Panama, my practical gland whispered to me, "Don't do it." Once the purchase was made, he played with the fit. No matter which way he turned it, he looked as if he were balancing a bamboo fishing coracle on a disappearing head. As we rejoined Eric, with delicacy, I asked Cowboy to consider giving up the gringo bull's-eye on his head before we boarded the southbound bus the next morning.

On the drive back to Mexico City, Eric gave me a graduate student's view of the U.S (elaborated on in later correspondence): "My feeling is that the U.S. government is always telling other governments, including Mexico, what to do, even though they don't have the moral right to do so. Your politicians talk about the drug traffic coming from Mexico, but they never mention the gun traffic from the north to Mexico. The U.S. likes to be in someone else's business, without actually knowing what is going on. But since they have money and power, it doesn't matter that they are ignorant."

"Why do you think the Mexico City audience at the recent Miss Universe pageant booed Miss America?" I asked.

"Miss America's beauty and physical perfection are a symbol of what the U.S. represents themselves as. So, they booed her, and when she fell down, then got back up smiling, that showed that she was not perfect. They booed her again. It was a funny situation, and since she represents our neighbor to the north, it was an opportunity to point out a symbol of an imperfection of the U.S. It wasn't very hospitable, and I didn't agree with it. I'm not anti-American, and I don't judge people by what country they are from. It's not like you can choose where you are born."

A few blocks from the hostel, Eric dropped us at Sanborns on Avenue Madero, near the Alameda Central. Opened by two California brothers over a century ago, the blue and white tiled building, a former palace, has been a century-old, archetypical Mexico City gathering spot for local elites and the avant-garde. Even Emiliano Zapata and his rebel forces, bandoliered and holding rifles during the Revolution, had breakfast in Sanborns. From the main dining room at street level to the upper balcony, the plaster walls are awash in boldly drawn murals, painted by a contemporary of Diego Rivera's. The waitresses dressed in something like the sunflowers in the Wizard of Oz. Stylish patrons, *boulevardiers*, imbued with airs of politesse and proprietary, caught my eye in their blue berets, black cravats, white linens and glittering rebozos. They ordered demitasses and European desserts, a small slice of another era it seemed. On the other hand, as dusty, denim wearing blow-ins, we were drowsily sated after knocking back several preprandial cervezas, a healthy bowl of pozole verde, and heaping plates of chilaquiles. We had an early bus to catch.

Zapotecs and Zapatistas

Chapter Two

SLEEP CAME IN BRIEF SNATCHES our last night at the hostel. My room gave on to the stairwell, which echoed everyone's late night comings and goings. So, when the bus pulled out at seven, I was unusually bleary-eyed. We were headed southeast to Oaxaca, home of the Zapotec and Mixtec Indigenes, west of the Isthmus of Tehuantepec. Before clearing the city's belt of misery, the driver switched on *Sniper II*, with Tom Berenger. I cracked a book while Cowboy and a crowd of men in white straw hats behind us took in the flick, a napalm-in-the-morning kind of start. Four women slept on the front row, wrapped like mummies in rough gray wool. A dark-skinned man sat next to me, wearing a Los Angeles Dodgers cap. Cheerily, he sang to himself for the eight-hour ride. He must have been going home, or away from somewhere less pleasant. Without common language, as if two autistics were meeting, we exchanged uncertain smiles.

Before long, fertile valleys gave way to mountains and again to valleys and so on. Burros plowed the fields, pulled carts to make-shift markets, encircled by whitewashed adobe walls with boldly scrawled advertisements. This breadbasket of corn, cabbage, peppers, cilantro, maguey, beans, squash, tomatoes, chocolate, and lush alfalfa represented an ancient cycle, a symbol of sustenance, of faith, of life from birth to earth, yes, a painterly rhythm of human geography. Pitching into this timeworn pace of life are goat herders, pig tenders, corn grinders, armadillo hunters, sheep shearers, bread makers, milkmaids, potters, weavers, vaqueros, moonshiners, tasks all blessed by a man of the cloth.

Tractors were rare. Bony horses, scrawny cattle, scattered herds of goats and sheep grazed in small plots. A truckload of chickens, another of hogs, slowed traffic as we threaded our way through fields of coffee. Water towers, palm and mango trees and church steeples stood tallest among the valley's *el pueblos*, or villages. Forlorn ridge-lines leapt up from each side, edged in purple.

At a snail's pace, we curled up the Sierra Madres. The landscape slowly turned incandescent. Those purple ridges morphed into burnt umber, their dry immensity swallowing everything like the ravages of some biblical drought. Uninhabited here, deep *baranches* became hot holes of desiccated river beds, of spindly stalks of cactus, salting the parched earth like skull-and-crossbones warnings. The inhospitable terrain between these valleys gave birth to the diverse Indian groups of Oaxaca, each developing in relative isolation.

Corkscrewing down into the Valley of Teotitlan, where one of the world's oldest farming cultures evolved, pine trees, purple jacaranda, fallow cotton fields and blond plots of maize formed a timeless patchwork. If Mesopotamia bloomed around wheat, it was here that corn rose up as king, domesticated from wild grass around 9,000 years ago. Side by side, in the same moment, beans grew bountifully in the wilds of the region. Mingling the two proteins made for a life-supporting diet. It wasn't, however, until 3,000 years ago that the process of nixtamalization was developed, taking a solution of water and lime and breaking down corn into flour for tortillas. Corn tortillas and beans, linchpin staples, have stood the test of time throughout Mesoamerica.

Charles V of Spain granted Don Hernando Cortes the title of Marquis of Oaxaca, and with that the best of this temperate valley's land. It turns out Cortes had wheedled from his earliest meeting with

Montezuma that the Aztec's treasures of gold were mined in Oaxaca. Thus the "curse of gold" was introduced, which like oil today, attracts those who want to extract and exploit, but not develop. As they say in Africa: "When elephants stampede the grass gets trampled." A half a millennium later, land tenancy disputes, a legacy of the curse, are rife in Oaxaca.

Oaxaca's Spanish square was bustling on this late afternoon, albeit well-guarded with flak-jacketed soldiers armed with automatic weapons on every corner. All freshly washed in primary colors, the casas, posadas, cafés, palaces and cosmopolitan boutiques of Oaxaca spilled forth as vividly-hued as a heap of M&Ms. We settled on twenty-dollar rooms at an aging posada off the zocalo, discounted because of recent rioting and bloodshed. The rooms gave way to a wrought iron balcony that faced the Moorish domes of Iglesias de La Compania. An Indigenous sax player stood before the 16th century church on the sidewalk, echoing riffs down the street, the grace notes of Oaxaca.

Only two months before, members of the Oaxaca People's Popular Assembly—made up of the teacher's union and a minority of revolution-minded Marxists—torched buildings and vehicles, barricaded streets with piles of burning tires, threw rocks, brandished clubs and sprayed graffiti like drunken muralists. At one point, black-ski-masked protesters smashed windows at the American Consulate.

Though still being washed and sandblasted away, the graffiti staining the plaza walls, "Assassin" or "Get Out, Ulises," was directed at the heavy-handed tactics of Oaxaca's Governor Ulises Ruiz. A life-size papier mache helicopter was hung in the zocalo, in front of the governor's palace, with an effigy of the governor propped up in the bubbled cockpit. The tail piece was splattered in silver paint that read "Ulises 666," an apocalyptic biblical reference.

The demonstration turned bloody when Governor Ruiz ordered tear gas canisters dropped from helicopters into the zocalo where protesters were encamped. As police stormed the square and

51

randomly pummeled tents, their actions caused one victim, a pregnant teacher, to miscarry. Then all hell broke loose: Federal troops were called in, and martial law was imposed. When the smoke cleared, more than 130 protesters were arrested, and thirteen were shot and killed by police.

What's more, a New York-based American journalist, Bradley Roland Will, was gunned down with two shots to the chest from a nine-millimeter Beretta (made in America). Will was there in sympathy with the protesters, filming the melee. Witnesses said government-backed paramilitary thugs were responsible. As with the thirty-eight other unsolved murders of journalists in Mexico, that have occurred over the past year and a half, the case has been turned on its head: Nothing is the way it appears.

Corrupt creole politicians and copper-faced Indigenes clashing in Oaxaca are of no surprise, but the ninety percent drop in tourism has hurt the average family. Oaxacans have hastily recovered, however, repainting the town, repairing the damaged buildings, restarting their lives. Bullet-pocked buildings are now tourist attractions. Having suffered many an earthquake, as well as social upheaval, they know about starting over, about living an uneasy truce.

❂ ❂ ❂

Cowboy disappeared in pursuit of paintings, as Oaxaca is home to many of Mexico's best artists. Next to the plaza, I finished a repast of protein-rich fried grasshoppers, or *chapulines*, spiced with chili sauce, wrapped in corn tortillas, and washed down with a cerveza. Recharged, I sprang up from the balcony terrace, with fresh legs, for a stroll.

As the light shifted, the plaza's impressionist daubs of yellow acacia and purple jacaranda, which I had been admiring, faded from spring glory into silhouettes of darkness. The night air was crisp, the moon shone luminous through the lofty treetops of the Indian laurels. Beyond, Sirius, the brightest star, linked to the cosmic jaguar cycle, traversed the heavens, as dependable as seasons and tides.

Dusky-faced Zapotec (ancient Oaxacan Indian culture) women, with babies slung to their backs and baskets teetering on their heads, edged into this nightly scene, their teeth sparkling white. Mestizo couples, donning their city clothes, modest but attractive, engaged in the evening *paseo*, a courtship ritual, holding hands, canoodling and circling repetitiously. Vanilla-skinned backpacker chicks casually coupled and promenaded with dark-faced Zapotec boys, their hair thick and dark as night. *Ambulantes*, ancient Indian crones, worked the crowd, table-hopping, exerting their seniority for turf rights, peddling plastic-wrapped nut candy, fried grasshoppers, onyx jewelry, and hand-dyed weavings.

A cascade of cheap music, the purest of Mexican fun, fell around me like an improvised carnival: combos with wooden marimbas, mariachi trios, accordion and trombone soloists, and dueling trumpets from each corner of the plaza. Jugglers, clowns, and cotton candy peddlers materialized like props among the colonnades, cobbled streets and cathedrals. Zestful organ grinders busked on the street corners. A full orchestra played jaunty folk melodies in the pavilion in the park. *La Cucaracha*, a popular Mexican Revolution-era tune about a cockroach that couldn't walk, sung *fortissimo*, got the locals dancing and harmonizing and snapping their fingers like castanets. The sounds of gay abandon.

From sushi and Sangria, Catalan filets and calzone pizza, to tacos and tequila, mole and martinis, there was food and drink for all palates. Pony-tailed, white-haired expatriate men, escapists of some ilk, lurked like Father Time in the outdoor cafés. They didn't appear to be of the crowd, but more engaged in a perpetual ritual of people watching.

An eighty-something man stood tall but frozen, parting a fast-flowing wave of the evening's paseo. Unlike a traffic cop, he wasn't gesturing, nor was he dressed for the job. He wore a sleeveless blue sweater, a red-pinstriped short sleeve shirt, khaki shorts and white knee socks, with sandals. British, I thought to myself. He seemed to

53

have jumped off the pages of a Graham Greene novel. He was handsome, even distinguished, but more importantly, he struck me as someone who would know the names of the big trees (Indian laurels) encircling the plaza.

"Hey there, do you know what these trees are? I asked, pointing to their gnarly trunks.

Puzzled by my sudden arrival, then the odd question, he glanced at the laurels and back at me, before saying, with a hint of an English public-school accent, "They are the lungs of the world." Pausing, cocking his head back in a quizzical manner, he added, "Why, are you in agriculture?

"No, I'm not, just a traveler. How 'bout you?"

Max's father was German and mother British. After World War II the family migrated to California from London. Sixty years later, his mannerisms are British, his heart is in pre-Hitler Germany, and his soul is Marxist.

Max was never clear about his life's work, other than saying he was an anti-war activist during the Vietnam years. As our conversation drifted, when I mentioned Castro, he perked up and said, "Oh, have you been to Cuba?"

"Yes, four years ago. And you?"

"I was there in '62," he said. "I remember thinking *Bravo! I lived to see the Revolution!* I traveled through Mexico to get to Havana on that trip, but once in Cuba Castro put me in detention for six weeks. I was in with the 'usual suspects,' as they say in *Casablanca*. Get it? Get it? Castro thought we were CIA. He was worried about another invasion and there we were. Looking back, it was natural for him to think that way."

"So, are you a communist?" I asked.

Shushing me, he said, "That's a bad word in America. But yes, Rosa Luxemburg and Karl Liebknecht are my heroes. Do you know them?"

54

"Rosa, yes, but can't recall Karl."

"They founded the Communist Party of Germany, edited the *Red Flag* newspaper and were assassinated by right wing death squads," he said. "You do know that Marx never intended for Russia to be the one—it was eighty percent rural peasants. The revolution was meant to occur in industrial Germany. Rosa and Karl were there to lead it, but instead we got a failed economy, and then Hitler and the Nazis." Refreshing his lungs with a deep breath, he then said, "Nazis, you know, were the iron hoop around the collapsing barrel of capitalism. Get it? Get it?"

We talked for an hour. As we were saying so long, I told Max that I hoped he shook the cough he had complained of. He returned the pleasantry, wishing me success with my search for the name of the trees, adding, "Capitalism has done the environment in. It will end the world someday."

Church bells rang, fireworks banged, while the mariachis played on. I went to bed. The day had flown by as in a dream.

Early the next morning, Cowboy and I waited on the south side of the plaza in front of the Government Palace, the center of political life in Oaxaca. The palace doors were shuttered at this hour. Within, I was told by a passerby practicing his English, that behind its balcony windows, centered with ruddy-colored crosses, the bold, neo-Aztec murals of Arturo Garcia Bustos, a contemporary of Diego Rivera, adorn the walls.

The plaza was eerily quiet and empty, the *laurels de India* forlorn. The shared van we were awaiting arrived with two skimpily-clad eighteen-year-old Dutch girls, students who had been living in Monterrey for a year to learn Spanish. In fact, they spoke four languages. We were all headed to the Zapotec ruins at Monte Alban.

After introductions and pleasantries, they told me of all the American factories in Monterrey. To their surprise, I asked them what those Monterrey Mexicans thought of Americans. Reluctantly, probably embarrassed, they responded together in a half-laugh, "You don't want to know."

"Please, you're not going to hurt my feelings."

"They don't like Americans and I don't know why," said the taller one. "For no reason they called our roommate from Chicago 'trash can.' Don't ask me why, maybe Bush. They were just mean to her and she did nothing. They even say we smoke grass because we are from Holland. We don't do that."

Atop Monte Alban, with a sweeping view of the confluence of three valleys, the four of us pitched in with a thrown-together group of American leftists: a mid-sixties political novelist and his wife; a real estate broker from New York (we share close mutual friends); a dilettantish forty-something woman from Cape Cod, wrapped in the local weave and adorned in turquoise jewelry; a former journalist and her husband, and a khaki-casual research engineer in his midseventies recently retired from Livermore Laboratories in California. The engineer was not happy about the major *Star Wars* contract that his former employer had just won from the Department of Defense. He made it clear that his work there in magnetics was unrelated to the weapons program, while his wife borrowed a page from Max (the old Marxist) as she piped up about capitalist greed and damage to the environment. Aside from the Dutch students, everyone I met here, in this post-riot tourist slump, were American leftists. This compounded my sense of the obvious that Oaxaca wasn't Cancun (or Kansas). Yet, on this day, we were all here for the cultural artifacts and history, not the politics. Our guide was a young Oaxacan grad student in history named Jorge.

⊙ ⊙ ⊙

In the era of Pericles's Athens, around 500 B.C., Zapotec architects engineered the flattening of Monte Alban. Then, after constructing crude stone edifices for residences, they turned Monte Alban into the Mt. Olympus of Mexico, home to 30,000 Zapotecs. Based on the cardinal points, and astronomically inspired, with an open view to the skies, the Zapotec architects centered everything on the *Gran Plaza*, a blond grassy common of ceremonial altars, pyramids, palaces, tombs and stelae.

In *Beyond the Mexique Bay*, Aldous Huxley wrote in the mid-thirties of Monte Alban's architectural magic:

> The most convincing way of proving that a given place is holy, is to make it so grand and so beautiful that when they see it, people catch their breath with astonishment and awe. Fine architecture is one of the visible embodiments of mana. It is a manifestation of the 'beauty of holiness,' of the beauty that is holiness. The Zapotecs knew all this so well that here, at Monte Alban, they allowed nothing to get in the way of the architects. Here should be no hole-and-corner sacred place, no slummy confusion of little shrines and temples; but one huge architectural complex informed from end to end by a single artistic idea and overwhelmingly impressive, as only a unified work of art can be.

Not much has changed since Huxley's time, yet we were seeing less than ten percent of what archaeologists believe to be buried here. Today, the upper slopes are shaded with wild cotton trees, yellow acacia and purple jacaranda. And a few miles down the road is the famous *Tule* tree, which sprouted over 2,000 years ago. Young Zapotec men played a soccer-style game on Monte Alban's centrally located ball court, manicured like an English pitch with sloped stone sides. These ancients used a rubber ball, but could only move it with their hips, shoulders, knees and elbows. Winning was all important, Jorge told us, as the losers were sacrificed to the gods.

Next to the ball court we had to fend off a gauntlet of tourist-starved Indians selling Zapotec idols. Most of their curios were partly caked with dirt as if freshly plucked from the sacred ground. On the west side of the plaza, passing a sacrificial altar where the unfortunate ballplayers found their way was Los Danzantes (or Temple of the Dancers). The temple's bas relief of fanciful male figures carved on stone slabs were probably not of dancers. According to Jorge, their pained expressions and contorted bodies suggest they were prisoners of war, or perhaps even dead.

Rulers of this highly organized, priest-dominated culture commanded from the Jaguar Throne. Today their tombs pock the north end of Monte Alban like a beehive of former plenty. The tombs were not open to us, but their contents of gold, amber, turquoise, silver, and alabaster can be found in the local museums and churches. Carved on these tomb walls, I was told, were ancient Zapotec hieroglyphs, long ago deciphered and phoneticized into a written language. This would make the Zapotec dialect, Jorge said, among the world's oldest extant languages.

❂ ❂ ❂

The Dutch girls caught a bus down the mountain in search of the ancient Tule tree and all the eternal mysteries it embodies. Returning to Oaxaca, I joined the Livermore Lab engineer and his journalist wife for a late breakfast on the plaza. Together they fretted about the false hope capitalism had given their ancestors, who left their environmentally-friendly farms for better lives and a better world for their kids. Now what? they asked.

An hour on, they left for their Spanish lessons. I hadn't taken ten steps when a white-haired lady wearing a blinding yellow dress and hoisting a red umbrella for shade waved me down as if we were old friends. She then proceeded to spit out sentences lightning fast. The upshot, I gathered, was that she was recruiting me as a customer to join her daily walking tour of Oaxaca.

Yet another progressive, Linda Ridgeway had lived in Cambridge, Massachusetts, the place I called home, for twenty years. She arrived in Mexico seven years ago for dental work, which was cheaper to do in Oaxaca, including travel costs, than in the U.S. She never left, cobbling together a life as an artist and photographer. She donates the proceeds from the city tours to an Indigenous charity, but uses the tours to introduce travelers to her paintings and photos.

In cityscape treasure troves like Oaxaca, I prefer roaming the streets, guided 'by eye and by fancy,' but Linda's enterprising boldness was hard to dismiss. So, I joined her. We were standing in front of the Oaxaca Cathedral, built in Cortes's time. She began the one-woman cook's tour by explaining that the Zapotec craftsmen, reluctant to abandon their pagan idols, had secretly inserted a carved block image of their fertility god just above the foundation of the cathedral. And to solve the mystery of the Holy Ghost, which puzzled would-be converts, Dominican priests accommodated: They ordered a dove to be carved high on the façade, between the bell towers.

At the time, Linda explained, many Zapotecs were saved from an early death in Cortes's mines because of the growing demand for cochineal, a natural red dye extracted from parasite insects infesting local cactus plants. Its popularity in medieval Europe rivaled that of the ancient Tyrean purple of the Phoenicians. The price of cochineal was quoted on European stock exchanges until the 19th century, after artificial dyes were introduced.

We passed through exquisite Old World-style colonial churches, with glass cases displaying the crucified Jesus, faster than most can walk from Baskin-Robbins to Best Buy in a mall. Dark-skinned, stylishly dressed Madonnas occupied the transepts of the chapels, "Virgins with alegria," Linda said. She told the story of the "Whiskey Priest," the dissolute Oaxaca-based padre and protagonist of Graham Greene's *The Power and the Glory*. Among other vices, the Whiskey Priest always stashed a flask of brandy in his robes, frittered away church coffers on French wine, slept with parishioners, and fathered at least one child. And then there were the "Holy Snitches," attorney generals in charge of identifying pagans and coercing their conversion. Zapotec dissidents retaliated by assassinating them. On a visit here four centuries later, Pope John Paul II beatified the Holy Snitches.

A block from the zocalo was Mercado Juarez. At a corner entrance Indians squatted in the dust selling mangoes and papayas, artfully arranging them in perfect pyramids. Nearby a young woman peddled fried grasshoppers, raking in pesos like autumn leaves. As I raised my camera, without warning she threw a handful of the tasty repast in my face. Safe to say I had never been pelted with a handful of chili-flavored grasshoppers. When I snickered in embarrassment, this angered her more. She pelted me again. "De-caff, baby," I mumbled, while skedaddling behind Linda into the market, where customized Catholicism was in full bloom.

Taking up vast shelf space was a crowded gallery of Santa Muerta (Black Saint) statues, papier mache and wooden carvings of cadavers and ghoulish men in priest robes. These images, as Linda explained, protect the drug lords, pimps and prostitutes: Do a drug deal, shoot a cop, turn a trick, have a chat with Mr. Bones, take communion, all is forgiven…start over. The garishly varnished Judas dolls are worshipped here as anti-heroes, not to be burned or exploded on Good Friday as mainstream tradition has it.

In the more garden-variety genre of devotional carvings, one popular shop sold life-sized statues of a curly-headed, breechclothed, toddling baby Jesus. He was pink-skinned, powdered and postured like a Happy Buddha. While we were in the store two of the baby Jesus carvings were bought by older couples, both of whom cooed like daffy grandparents. For reasons not obvious, the bigger-than-life statues of Jesus-at-Calvary weren't moving so fast this Lenten season; they were marked down forty percent. "Only in Mexico," Linda said, "a discounted Jesus!"

Across the street from the Church of San Felipe Neri was the former home of Porfirio Diaz, the ruthless dictator of Mexico, whose oppressive tactics led to the Revolution. But for a brightly painted green door, and a token street given his name, there was not much in Oaxaca to remember this famous native son.

More romantically, Benito Juarez, Mexico's most beloved leader and the only full-blooded Indian ever to be president, was married here in San Felipe Neri church. Orphaned at three, Juarez was an illiterate shepherd boy from the nearby village of San Pablo Guelatao. Until age twelve, when he moved in with a sister in Oaxaca, he was not able to speak Spanish. A lay Franciscan businessman identified his eagerness to learn and placed him in seminary. Afterward he studied law and became a judge, but fell out with the military dictator Santa Anna (of Alamo fame), and went into exile in New Orleans. Once Santa Anna abdicated in 1855, Juarez repatriated to lead the liberal reform movement. Among other issues, it sought to rein in the Catholic church's influence. Churches closed and priests and nuns were forced to stop wearing their cassocks and habits in public, a practice that only ended in 1993.

Juarez admired the U.S constitution for its separation of church and state. Although he confiscated land from the wealthy for redistribution, he attempted to model Mexico on the capitalist economy of the U.S. He was Mexico's Abraham Lincoln, himself a contemporary and an admirer of the reform-minded Juarez.

When President Juarez announced a moratorium on foreign debt payments, Napoleon III sent in troops, backed by Mexican conservatives. As a war on reform took hold between liberals and conservatives, Napoleon III backed the liberal younger brother of the Hapsburg Emperor of Austria, whom he anointed as Maximilian I to rule Mexico. At the same time, Juarez warmed to the U.S., which invoked the Monroe Doctrine, throwing its considerable weight against the occupation of Mexico by a European power. Lincoln supplied weapons to Juarez's government-in-exile. In a desperate move, Maximilian offered Juarez amnesty and the office of prime minister. Juarez, however, wanted nothing to do with this failed attempt at monarchy.

Back in France, with Prussia spoiling for a fight, interest in Mexico disappeared. Maximilian's forces were soon weakened. In 1867, he was defeated, captured and sentenced to death by a military court. A victorious Juarez refused worldwide appeals, from the U.S. and throughout Europe, to commute Maximilian's sentence. Juarez was intent on sending a message to the monarchies of Europe, one laden with unspoken reprisal for Cortes's invasion, for the deaths of Montezuma and Cuauhtémoc, for the fall of the Aztecs 350 years before. Honoring his last request, at least as Hollywood has portrayed it, "La Paloma" played as Maximilian was executed by firing squad. Five years on, Juarez keeled over dead while working at his desk in the National Palace. Conservative Porfirio Diaz would succeed him four years later.

❂ ❂ ❂

Linda showed me the bullet holes in the Basilica de la Soledad, said to be from Maximilian's French army. As entertaining as her satirical swing through Oaxaca's Catholic past had been, I was cooked on Spanish churches, so we took a shady spot among the *helados* vendors, their ice creams made in old wooden barrels.

Then bang, bang, bang, a volley of shots rang above the rising cacophony of an emerging procession of men and women. Most were donning white straw hats as they charged into the basilica courtyard: It was a Friday Lent celebration, one of those unexpected fiestas that Mexico, and notably Oaxaca, is famous for. Bottle rockets swished by and popped in the four directions. Senoras with hand-woven baskets of hard candies on their heads showered the frothing crowd with sweet tokens of Lent. Among a procession of church and municipal dignitaries, other celebrants carried stalks of flowers for the altar. A troupe of Paul Bunyan-sized papier mache figures, known as *cartoneria*, were hoisted about in the crowd as jokers, or even historical characters. Two such figures portrayed a freshly dressed Zapotec couple, a youthful Benito Juarez in a fancy *charro* costume and his child bride in a Tehuana dress. Some twenty minutes later, as the tumult of music, fireworks and screaming faded, and the candy had been expended, the straw-hatted crowd turned indifferent, milled around and drifted off bathically.

Cowboy had disappeared, looking for "mule art" oil paintings to adorn the bunkhouse walls of his newly acquired mule ranch in Colorado. We met up in front of Oaxaca Cathedral with our bags. A street show of folk-art painting was underway on the south side of the cathedral. Four artists had stretched their white drawing paper between four sets of makeshift wooden stands. They rapidly traced their images and then let go with cans of spray paint: a Madonna, a mule, a futuristic space ship. They may well have been the same graffiti artists who recently stained the walls of Oaxaca in the heat of protest.

Around the corner a stage had been set up. A *banda* of trumpets and trombones kicked out the jams, blasting the afternoon hush to the top of Monte Alban. Each musician of the all-male band donned a white suit, a black open-collared shirt, white bucks, and sported gelled black hair. They were flanked by armed police in flak jackets. A blank-faced crowd of Oaxacans bunched up at the stage. Others listened from tables along the plaza. The rhythmic soundscape of nocturnal Oaxaca began afresh, as we boarded the bus, off to San Cristobal.

Sleep was fitful, screeching airbrakes, a wheezing engine, the relentless murmur of voices, prevailed through the night. It was eight the next morning before the bus switch-backed down the foggy highlands into San Cristobal. The surrounding hillsides were blanketed in barrios of displaced Indians, many now evangelized by American missionaries. Rubbing the grout from our eyes, we stumbled the short distance up a rain-drenched street from the bus station to the plaza. On the corner of the Spanish square stood an older Canadian couple, all patched up in maple leaves, as if U.N.

workers. With a State Department warning in place, there were few Americans arriving in these parts.

Gray slants of rain aside, San Cristobal awoke in techno-color. Washed in pastels, stucco homes and Spanish churches were as garish, they say, as the feathers of a macaw. The Zapata Café and Bar, just opening with its first customers, was painted a bright crimson, with a black and white portrait of its namesake, Emiliano Zapata, sculpted above the door. Posters of Che Guevara were plastered everywhere like campaign signs. If alive, I thought, Che could have life tenure as mayor in this Indian-colonial town. We were in Zapatista country.

❂ ❂ ❂

Emiliano Zapata was born in the central state of Morelos in 1879 and rose to fame during Mexico's Revolution. He was mission-bound to restore land to peasants, as laid out in his controversial "Plan of Ayala." It was Zapata who minted the rally cry still used by Indigenes today, "Tierra y Libertad" (Land and Freedom). As commander of the Liberation Army of the South, he and Pancho Villa's armies (Zapatistas and Villistas) controlled most of Mexico. After Dictator Porfirio Diaz abdicated, a succession of unpopular dictators—Francisco Madero, Victoriano Huerta, Venustiano Carranza— took power only to be ousted by competing factions. The pendulum of power between landlords and peasants had the play of an unsteady hangman's rope. In 1915, Zapata and Villa took control of Mexico City, but with no political solution for Mexico to move forward they too were ousted.

From the capital, Zapata and his army of Zapatistas fled to the mountains, where they pursued an armed, anarchic campaign for land reform. After years of guerilla fighting, however, the Zapatistas were fractured and exhausted. Even so, Zapata refused to put down his arms, believing as Mao did, that power grows out of the barrel of a gun. Zapata was eventually lured into an ambush, and like Villa a few years later, was riddled with bullets and murdered.

In death, a national hero was born, a martyr. His legacy was re-vived on January 1, 1994, the day the North American Free Trade Agreement took effect, received by modern-day Zapatistas like hurled Olympian thunder. Led by a university professor-turned-Marxist revolutionary, Subcommander Marcos (Rafael Sebastian Guillen Voconte), Zapatistas commandeered San Cristobal. Recently formed *ejidos*, communal land holdings, were said to be under threat by development-minded conservative capitalists. Couched in Marxist rhetoric, Marcos, always clad in a black balaclava and smoking a pipe, had denounced globalization and railed against President Clinton, the motive force behind NAFTA. He also had nothing but scorn for beggar-thy-neighbor tactics of American agriculture ventures that would undercut and marginalize small farmers in Chiapas.

Marco's uprising of 300 militants was quickly quelled by the Mexican army, but only after 150, mostly civilians and Zapatistas, had been killed. The rebels fled to the Lacandon jungle of east Chiapas, where Marcos launched propaganda warfare by Internet. Paramilitary fighters of the ruling PRI (Institutional Revolutionary Party), who until interrupted by the election in 2000 of Vicente Fox, ruled Mexico for eight decades, retaliated with a campaign of intimidation, wiping out forty-five civilians in one Indian village. Thousands were forced to flee the terror to the hillside barrios of St. Cristobal, where they remain even today.

Zapatistas countered by, among other village-based tactics, building roads, bridges, and community centers, keeping Indigenous rights in the political arena. After repeated warnings to foreign land-owners, in 2003 the Zapatistas took over a nearby American farm catering to eco-tourism. Mexican military and police stood down, while Subcommander Marcos decried tourism and American invest-ment, saying that development schemes would turn the region into "an amusement park for foreigners." After three decades of NAFTA (as succeeded by the USMCA), American-subsidized corn has flooded the Mexican market, causing local prices to plummet as rural poverty, food insecurity, and migration soared.

More recently, in a failed attempt to mobilize Mexico's leftists, Subcommander Marcos crusaded across the country by motorcycle. As ever, the Indigenous, communal farms continue to unnerve Mexico's conservatives and U.S. commercial interests.

Cowboy and I found rooms in the Hotel Santa Clara, next door to where the Canadian couple had nested and held ground like flag poles. Built by the Spanish ruler of Chiapas, once part of the Kingdom of Guatemala, the wide-planked wooden floors, thick, iron-strapped doors, chilly rooms with stacked-rock fireplaces, and a columned, flagstone courtyard with caged macaws, spoke of erstwhile colonial life here in San Cristobal. After chucking our bags and purchasing a bus ticket on to Palenque, we hired a truck and driver to take us to Chumala, an Indigenous village of faith healers an hour's drive away.

Circling the iron bandstand in the plaza, we found our way to the front of the nearby Santa Clara Cathedral, where we had agreed to be picked up. Postcard images of balaclava-clad Zapatistas, rifles at the ready, were sold on the sidewalk like ex-votos. The heavy rain turned to light mist. In front of the Spanish-era cathedral was an effigy of George Bush portrayed as Hitler. Locals ho-hummed it, passing without pause. Two Dutch tourists snapped photos.

Bishop Samuel Ruiz Garcia, who spoke four Maya dialects, served here for forty years, an empathetic voice for the underdog. Like many Latin American theologians of the time, he preached through a lens of "liberation theology" which ran the political spectrum from social justice advocacy to no daylight between Marxism and Christianity. Pope John Paul II detested liberation theology, claiming that it incited leftist politics among the 1.4 million Indians in Chiapas (and throughout Latin America). After the Zapatista attacks following the trade agreement in 1994, Bishop Ruiz was accused of provoking the uprising. Many pro-government Indian landowners despised Ruiz. Before retiring at age seventy-five, he had taken to wearing a bullet proof helmet when in the countryside.

◎ ◎ ◎

Robert, in his late fifties, arrived with the pickup truck and driver, Rafael, a local Indian. Rafael spoke English, Spanish, and several dialects of Tzeltal, a Maya language. Robert hailed from Montreal and had lived for ten years in Mexico City, managing a family toy manufacturing business. His first few words in English revealed that was his first language, followed by French and Spanish. I gathered that Robert travels often and widely and along the way picked up a knack for offending people.

"Where's your maple leaves?" I blurted from the back seat, a prickly effort at getting him to acknowledge us gringos.

For the moment, this seemed to lighten him up. He laughed, turned to face me, and said, "When I backpacked the Hippy Highway [Istanbul to Katmandu] in the early '70s, everyone from Montreal told me to wear the maple leaves, but after a few months on the road, I took them off. I was traveling with Americans, and haven't worn them since."

Yet he kept talking about us as gringos, throwing an aimless thumb toward the back seat, while speaking in Spanish to Rafael. It was as if we weren't present. Turns out Robert made it up as he went. It was indeed important to him to quickly be identified as Canadian to all we met. Whether out of fear or patriotism, it puzzled me. We weren't in any danger, as an American might be in a few Middle East hotspots. We were all *touristas*, equally open prey to the artifices of local grifters and hangers-on.

Robert did affect an air of authority on all matters Mexican, so Cowboy took the bait and asked him how "gringo" entered their lexicon.

"When Yankee soldiers invaded Mexico City, locals responded by shouting two words at the imperialists—'green' (for the uniforms) and 'go,'" he said. To reinforce his dark resentment of Americans, he assured us that noted historians back in Mexico City had informed him of this. "Go check for yourself. You'll see," he challenged us.

Robert was a talker, and prone to facile versions of reality. Turns out, the American armed services during Polk's war against Mexico had yet to adopt green uniforms; they wore blue at the time (which those historians Robert referred to would have known).

The true origin of "gringo" most likely predates the Mexican-American War by centuries, deriving from the Spanish word for Greek, *griego*. In Spanish, as well as English, Greek has been, even in Shakespeare's time, a metaphor for something difficult to comprehend. That said, it was first used in American literature in 1849, just after the Mexican-American War, by John Woodhouse Audubon, who wrote: "We were hooted and shouted at as we passed through, and called 'Gringoes.'"

So, the Spanish word *griego* was probably Mexican-ized, perhaps during or near in time to the Mexican-American War, to refer to their not-so-easily-comprehended northern neighbors. In addition to the anodyne usage of identifying U.S. citizens, the vernacular gringo often connotes negative feelings, such as making fun of the boss, of someone powerful, which I suppose was Robert's purpose in repetitively using the word.

As the conversation turned, Rafael told the story of a Spanish settlement in St. Cristobal, only moderately paraphrased. "They didn't bring wives to New Spain, but they did import 700 Aztec women to Chiapas. They were smart. This was a calculated breeding program, with the intent of dividing and conquering. Which they did: The region was cut up into seven municipalities, each represented by one of the Catholic orders—Dominican, Franciscan, Jesuit, Benedictine, and so on—each with its own tribal costume. Soon mestizos were ruling, and over time, were almost as common in St. Cristobal as Indigenes."

Before Chamula, we stopped in a Tzeltal-speaking Indian village. As a freak class with money, we were mobbed by Indian women flogging textiles and ex votos. Inside a wood-plank hut we were given short stools, the size used to milk cows, around a fire on an earthen floor. Two eleven-year-old girls made us corn tortillas over an open hearth, sprinkling goat cheese on top and pumpkin seeds to the side. For them, the flush of life had just begun. These crimson-cheeked, early adolescents would be brides in another two years, mothers of five in a decade. Their mama, not much older than twenty-five, poured us dusky-thimble shots of *posh*, a whiskey-derived sugarcane juice. Robert took his shot and acted out the Mexican version of cheers: *Arriba, abajo, al centro, para adentro* (Up, down, center, inside). It was not even mid-afternoon, and the tips of my ears were warm and tingling. We were model tourists, half-sloshed.

Chamula was covered in clouds, dark gray and unsettled. On one end of the market plaza was a white stucco Catholic church, said to have been built over 250 years ago. Men and women in heavy wool ponchos stood in front. This was no ordinary church, and these were not ordinary Christians. You didn't have to venture far beneath the surface to find a crazy quilt of Pashtun-like patriarchy and sub-Sahara African pagan sacrifice.

Rafael talked fast as we waited on the gatekeeper in a light mist at the church's double-wooden doors. "Priests only come here for baptisms, not for communion, confession or marriage. Men here are polygamists, and give bride prices of up to $5,000 for a thirteen or fourteen-year-old. They only pay $1,500 for a woman of twenty or more years. Just like Muslims, they can take as many wives as they can afford."

He paused before stating the obvious, "In Chamula, men have all the power." He continued, "The village patriarchs control the money. They often make loans to young men to purchase their brides. If the elders are not repaid, they sleep with the bride."

69

Photos were not allowed. It wasn't difficult, however, to develop vivid mental pictures of this primal clan and their superstitions. Standing stock still in sheer astonishment between the narthex and nave, before now, I imagined a witch's den to be mythical. But this sickroom haunt of medieval medicine men and women might capture the contours of such a woo-woo place.

The ceilings were tall and as open as a barn. Shadows flashed across the dusky slats like a stormy night sky. Resinous perfumed pine needles were strewn about the earthen floor. There were no benches or seats, only an open floor swept clean by the faith healers, or *curanderos*. While chanting madly, curanderos squatted among fields of trembling candles, which they lit obsessively, intensely, without cease, like junkies cooking down meth. This pagan ritual smacked of fire worship, of Druids, of dragons, the whole kit and caboodle of history's fire masters.

Most Catholic churches are dedicated to one or two saints, but here there were up to twenty-five, each adorned in holy garb, with reflectors on their chests to channel the healing spirit. Curative nuances aside, their idol-like aspects conjured a house of mirrors. A Mos Eisley spaceport town couldn't call forth a cast of characters so utterly weird.

John the Baptist took center stage at the altar. "In Chamula he is the favorite saint," Rafael explained, pointing to his aspect. "Even the cattle and sheep of the Spanish are worshipped here. Sheep are considered an incarnation of John the Baptist. Even so, when the sheep grow old and no longer produce wool, they are sold in the market."

It struck me that to be baptized here in Chamula was only the beginning of a life of artifice to fight off evil, always wary of anyone lurking outside the cocoon they had woven. It also felt that we had stumbled onto a puzzle piece: These were the descendants of Maya pagans, the animist holdouts from the Franciscan inquisitors, the ones who kept the faith, the ancestral emotions. Their forebears had necessarily blended with the Christian invaders to escape an early death, no different than the Middle East practice of "religious dissimulation" known as *taqiyya*—disguising beliefs in order to fit in. And like the "evil eye" found all over the Middle East, their world is full of black cats, all in the eye of the diviner.

In Chamula they still use the Maya calendar: eighteen months with twenty days in each month, then another five days, a unique number adopted by the healers. On the last day of that five-day month, locals take a pilgrimage to a sacred altar in the mountains. There, Rafael said, they fire-walk on burning straw to purify the body and mind.

We moved near the altar, standing next to a coffee-skinned female curandero covered in black wool. She was aged beyond her years, forty, but easily taken for sixty. She chanted and hummed like a chorus of ten monks, lit and spread lime green and orange candles in a ring of luminescence, and reached into her woven ixtle basket for bottles of Coke, Fanta and Sprite. She then poured and set aside a thimble-full of Sprite for her chosen saint. Time passed, the chanting grew louder, a sweet-and-foul odor of incense and smoked tapers suffused the church. The healer withdrew a photo of the patient from her basket, and rubbed it like a rabbit's foot with a chicken egg. Nearby another healer arrived and squatted with her tools for healing, taking the pulse of a six-year-old girl with dead doll eyes, frantically spreading white candles. Anon, a sinister fury of chanting charged the room in an atmosphere I imagined to be primal currents. Seven or eight curanderas followed their daemon, funneling and healing, circled by an orgy of trembling blazes, the hellish intensity of a Dante scene.

Then, as if from a magician's hat, the healer we were standing next to pulled from her woven basket a black-and-white chicken. Rafael color-coded the plumage for me, saying it meant something between "death and mildly sick." Rubbing the patient's picture about the chicken, thirty minutes lapsed before the curandero fumbled to find a whistle in a cardboard box next to her basket. She then sum-moned the healing spirit: wringing the chicken's neck and blowing hard on the whistle.

The black-and-white hen flopped for a couple of minutes in her lap before dying. According to Rafael, spoken with the calm of a clinician who had just watched an IV of antibiotics administered, "The patient in the picture has been cured. The disease had been transferred to the dead chicken, which the healer would soon bury." Silence fell over her. She sat motionless, staring vacantly. The impli-cation was that a successful exorcism had occurred. All of this was as hard to grasp as a handhold on the flashing shadows above.

The wooden church doors slammed shut behind us. The rain had stopped. I felt overcome by a suffocating feeling, stunned for the moment. Just watching all the witcheries had been a crucible or trial in itself. We crossed the street to the church commissary that spe-cialized in a candle trade for the faith healers. As if taking commun-ion, they offered us thimbles of posh. We each threw one back, then another, and another before I yelped, "oh, the sweet polarities."

A grandiose banner of Pope John Paul II hung above the door. Cowboy wondered aloud if the Pope had ever been to Chumala. The answer would probably be no, but there was another religious titan, one who in his day was as equally evolved and celebrated as the Pope and who arrived in Chiapas 1,600 years ago and took the Maya culture to its apogee. His name was Fire is Born.

Chapter Three

THE NEXT MORNING THE BUS was full of mostly locals, with a dozen or fewer French and Dutch backpackers, and no other Americans. Hanging around the station on a bicycle, however, there was one talkative, shivery, travel-fatigued compatriot in his mid-thirties, with a cascading brown beard, recalling the aspect of a Muslim fundamentalist. In our momentary encounter, the most coherent thought he imparted was that he had been living near Palenque for a month in the Lacandon jungle. "No one's gone where I've been," he told me. "There are boas everywhere." The man, docile enough, had the flesh-eating grin of a mongoose, seeming to have traveled beyond his own psychic frontier. I started to let him in on where I'd been. Maybe give him a shopping list, a chicken, a box of candles, a bottle of Sprite and woo-woo directions on how he could get rid of those snakes in his head. I let it go, though. Too hard to explain when you're on the trail of Fire is Born.

In the '90s, Highway 199 to Palenque, the ancient Maya city, was known for Zapatista holdups and banditos, but less so today…at least until early evening and night, the warnings say. It was six in the morning when we left the St. Cristobal bus station and began spiraling through the foggy defiles of east Chiapas. Traffic was scant. From one side to the other, a jungle canopy spread wildly along mocha brown rivers, flowing full from the seasonal rains. Along the way, straw-hatted farmers emerged from the forests with machetes and bags of chopped wood on their backs, both food and fuel demands were chipping at the edges of the jungle. Indigenous villages of wooden huts, with corrugated tin roofs and earthen floors, popped out of the ether. Camouflaged bunkers and a speed bump greeted us in a few of those villages, all bearing the face of poverty, but each generously populated with pigs and chickens, the landscape lush with mango, papaya, and banana trees, and the steep hillsides scored with the ubiquitous mosaic of Maya cornfields. Full of hothouse verdure and ripe for clear-cutting and cultivating coffee plantations, this region of peasant subsistence farms, for better or worse, defied the anthropologist's maxim that says, "The level to which a culture can develop is dependent upon the agricultural potentiality of the environment it occupies."

As the sun rose higher, the fog receded in misty waves, lighting up in an impressionist's dream patches of Mexican sunflowers, pink wildflowers lining the pastures, and purplish bougainvillea surrounding the kitchen gardens. Soon we were unloading for a pit stop in the market town of Ocosingo, a stronghold of Zapatistas.

During the '94 rebellion, which began the day NAFTA was signed, some of the worst bloodshed occurred in Ocosingo. Fifty rebels were killed. Though the Mexican army is garrisoned here, the Zapatistas continue to rid the area of outside influences by seizing expatriate properties, most famously the American-owned tourist destination Rancho Esmeralda. Fair to say, the Zapatista movement in Mexico is no more than the most recent episode of 450 years of anti-colonial sword-pointing.

Once out of Ocosingo, even as the driver careened down the pot-holed highway, the Indian man in the seat next to me never woke, sleeping with his head turned at an excruciating right angle. Miles out of Palenque we passed a sylvan meadow, jammed with more retired black and white police cars than trees, with a rusting single engine Cessna nearby. Best I could gather, we were in drug-trafficker country—DEA territory—and all those metal carcasses struck me as a local graveyard for the losers in the "war on drugs."

❂ ❂ ❂

As Cowboy and I shambled up to the guest house east of Palenque's bus station, the shirtless owner sang out, "*Buenas tardes!*" Upon hearing my reply, he then said, "Gringos, we don't see so many."

"Oh yeah?" I said "Who are your guests?"

"Dutch, German, French, Italian, Argentine," he told me. "Americans are afraid someone is hiding in the bushes." With that gibe, he let go of a mocking laugh, while raising his arms as if cradling a rifle. "Bush did that. So now gringos go to Cancun and Cozumel. But welcome, we have rooms."

Having worked up an appetite, we threw our bags in our rooms and hit the streets, looking for a *taqueria* along Palenque's Ave Juarez. Passing a Maya statue in the center of a three-way crossroads, on its busiest stretch, Ave Juarez has that Klondike feel of being thrown together overnight, a scrambling of curbside food peddlers and bars, bus ticket stalls, DVD hawkers and one Internet café. On this day the street was quiet, the petty retailers languid as lizards in the afternoon heat.

We came up on a Swiss couple on bicycles: he with a trailer the size of a dog house for his three-year-old son, his blond head sticking out from behind a waterproof mesh window and she with a map laid out across the handlebars and working out directions. Both were professional landscapers, they told us. They'd put together a stash for an extended, one-off adventure. From Palenque they were turning south to Guatemala, and then on to Panama, where they hoped to arrive in three to four months, but only if they cycled an average of three or four hours a day. They had spent seven months and $7,000 getting here, having started their journey in Vancouver. "If the money holds out, after Panama, we will go on through South America," he told me.

Watching the Swiss family pedal away, in a nearby taqueria we ordered beans and tortillas from a Maya girl in a woven skirt. A twenty-something couple who overheard us asked if we were Americans. Turns out, they were grad students at the University of West Virginia. He was here doing fieldwork for his thesis on the Zapatistas. After a week in Palenque, they had not met any other Americans, and were eager to talk. They told us what they knew about the many Maya ruins in the area before we jumped on a *colectivo* (small bus) with only a few hours left before the archaeological site closed. We hoped to arrive at the Guatemala border crossing the next evening.

❂ ❂ ❂

"Ancient inscriptions give the date as January 8, 378, and the stranger's name as Fire is Born," reported *National Geographic*. "He arrived in Waka, in present-day Guatemala, as an envoy from a great power in the highlands of Mexico." Fire is Born had followed our same path from Teotihuacan, the mysterious Aztec ruins we'd visited outside of Mexico City. He was like an aboriginal Caesar, though, arriving with shock troops, spear-throwers and obsidian-tipped javelins, there to conquer and expand his empire. "In the coming decades, his name would appear on monuments all across the territory of the Maya, the jungle civilization of Mesoamerica. And in his wake, the Maya reached an apogee that lasted five centuries."

The Maya's pre-classic roots go back 3,000 years to the time of Rameses the Great in Egypt. According to *National Geographic*, as the story goes, it was not until the convulsing arrival of Fire is Born that Maya began to prosper in the rain forest as city-states:

> The Maya built elegant multiroom palaces with vaulted ceilings; their temples rose hundreds of feet toward the heavens. Ceramics, murals, and sculpture displayed their distinctive artistic style, intricate and colorful. Though they used neither the wheel nor metal tools, they developed a complete hieroglyphic writing system and grasped the concept of zero, adopting it for everyday calculations. They

also had a 365-day year and were sophisticated enough to make leap-year-like corrections. They regularly observed the stars, predicted solar eclipses, and angled their cere-monial buildings so that they faced sunrise or sunset at par-ticular times of year.

For all their achievements, 20th century American archaeolo-gist, Sylvanus Morley, preferred to call the pre-Colombian Maya the "Greeks of the New World."

❂ ❂ ❂

Cowboy and I were the last to jump out of the colectivo. We had arrived at the entranceway to ancient Palenque, a place of geo-logical transition that rises like an Olympus from the coastal foothills and is surrounded by a mahogany canopy of dense jungle on the west-ern edge of the once great Maya empire. Palenque is a Spanish name, meaning "fortification," but the Maya called their city *Lakam Ha*, "Big Water," after the numerous springs that cascade from the limestone slopes of the Chiapas Mountains. In recognition of those limestone slopes, the Maya kingdom became known as *Bak*, or "Bone."

The primal cry of howler monkeys cracked the solitude, like sentinels for the dead at Palenque. We fell in with a Czech couple, both engineers, who spoke some Spanish and translated for the as-piring young Indigenous guide who followed us, providing a helpful framework of Maya lore.

The sky darkened as we climbed the eight levels of the Temple of Inscriptions, to the tomb of Pacal the Great, a ruler for sixty-eight years who oversaw the expansion of Palenque. Unlike other Maya kings, Pacal's tomb was placed inside the Temple of Inscriptions, rather than in a necropolis as in other Maya cities. He was a holy lord, or *kuhul ajaw*, a hereditary ruler, one who would have been in fashion in a feathered-green headdress and a cloak of turquoise. He kept the cosmic order, erected temples and palaces, stage-managed ritual fire ceremonies of commoners dancing and chanting in flowered-crowns, and commanded the defense against rival city-states with gamely, sandal-footed soldiers hoisting the *macuahuitl*, a wooden club with sharp obsidian blades.

That was another time. Palenque had been abandoned for centuries and consumed by the jungle when the Spanish arrived and reported dispersed communities of Maya living near their temples.

It wasn't until 1952 that a Mexican archaeologist went deep within the temple vault and opened Pacal's carved stone sarcophagus, which depicted his journey of death down the Milky Way Tree Road into the jaw of a serpent, the White-Bone-Snake of Xibalba, the Otherworld. Upon lifting the coffin lid, the archaeologist found the king's remains to be decorated in jade rings, beads, statues, and ear flares, and his face covered in a fabulous jade death mask, a mosaic of 340 pieces.

Jade, in Maya tradition, represented immortality. When the Spanish and Cortes arrived, they banned jade as a pagan symbol. Yet, like their Chumala cousins, the Maya never completely gave up their pagan gods, known here as the Palenque Triad—Maize God, Mirror God, and Lord Sun.

To prevent further damage to the galleries of murals and inscriptions, we were not allowed to enter as members of the public customarily did in ancient times. The tombs' hieroglyphic panels provided a dynastic history of the kingdom, given in *k'atuns*, or twenty Maya years (a vigesimal system versus the European decimal), describing the king's lineage through "time travel," back into the Neolithic mists. The inscriptions are said to be the longest continuous text from the classical period to survive intact, making the temple one of the greatest historical legacies in the Americas.

Recording time was an obsession of the Classical Maya. "Time came to be regarded as the sole lasting coinage for all earthly and celestial transactions," wrote Victor Perera in *Unfinished Conquest*. "The Mayas viewed the universe as a vast chain of interlinked time segments recurring in predetermined cycles, so that nothing was ever truly lost in their cosmos; nor, for that matter, was anything finally gained. The great wheel of time ground all earthly events, great and small, to a fine dust, whose grains germinated the seeds of the next cycle of creation."

The Maya's metaphysical concept of time recalled the infinity of Buddhism's endless cycles of rebirth: "…Astronomers represented zero as a seashell that symbolizes, alternatively, an end with no beginning, or a beginning without end," Perera explained. Time is circular, he summed up: not only is the past prologue, but the present and future as well.

A seasonal monsoon rain began to shower us. We hurried down the narrow, pyramidal steps, across the aqueduct, and up again into the palace courtyards, among the stucco reliefs. A whippet-thin young man standing beneath the astronomical tower, looking cooler than a cucumber by a factor of infinity, wearing a white-and-royal-blue-striped Zoot suit, with black tennis shoes and matching fedora set atop a head of long, reddish hair. That he was kitted out like some kind of rock star led Cowboy to strike up a conversation. He soon found out that the fly-dressed youngster, who turned out to be a butter smooth talker, had been donating his time to relief work in New Orleans for a year. When Cowboy scratched deeper, he discovered that before arriving in NOLA, his new buddy had been thrown in jail in Tulsa on various misdemeanor charges such as possession of pot and drunk and disorderly. I'm sure he thought he had just shocked two old guys, but as the skies opened into a frog choker, the three of us shook hands, and Cowboy parted by speaking some truth. "Goddamn, ain't this a coincidence, the only three gringos here at Palenque, and all three of us have been in an Oklahoma hoosegow."

The next morning, at Frontera Corozal, on the Usumacinta River, we loaded into a *lancha*, or thatched roof jon boat, for an hour's ride downriver to Yaxchilan, a rival city-state to Palenque. On the fecund, cultivated east side of the jade green waters was Guatemala. To the west were Mexico and the Lacandon jungle, home to over 4,000 plant species, 1,500 different trees, thirty-three percent of Mexican birds, butterflies out the wazoo, and 163 mammals, including pumas, spider monkeys, and the jaguar, or *balam*.

In Maya mythology, the jaguar is a revered symbol of authority. Often invoked as the patron god of cities, rulers wore the jaguar pelt and took the name Balam. What's more, in the Maya world view, opposites interpenetrate: illusion and reality, night and day, the living and the dead, earth and the spirit world. As such, the gods associated with the stealth and cunning of the nocturnal jaguar bridge these extremes.

It was mid-morning, and for the first time in three days, the skies were azure, the air light and crisp, the earth fresh washed. The sun path would have to arc higher before the bathers and village women washing clothes on the rocks would come down from their thatched huts on the Guatemala side. Topped in a flowering crown of spring yellow, lofty hardwoods, held dear by Tabasco timber merchants, grew abundantly along the river. Fishermen in small pirogues unfurled their nets, hawks and eagles wheeled above while cormorants swam in the strong current and dove near the shore.

In a camouflaged sandbag bunker dug in next to the buttressed roots of a towering ceiba, sacred to Maya and the country's national tree, Guatemalan government soldiers in red berets stood vigil, armed with automatic weapons. These were the elite special forces, the Jaguar Kaibiles. As a test of the Kaibiles' red meat fiber, their survival training includes taking along a pet dog, and after an extended, solitary stay in the bush, butchering and devouring man's best friend.

During much of the thirty-year Guatemalan civil war, these same shores were occupied by an Indigenous guerilla army. Then

80

and now, *contrabandistas*, smugglers and dope runners ford these waters with everything from Colombian cocaine and marijuana and Chinese fentanyl, to cheap Mexican petrol headed the opposite direction, to migrants from countries near and far going north to Gringolandia. In only a few short minutes, peeking out of the forest along the river banks, we had spotted four men, ragged looking from crawling and scrambling through thorn-bushes. According to the boatman, they were emigrants, searching for a safe crossing.

During the civil wars of Nicaragua, El Salvador and Guatemala from here south to Tapachula near the Pacific Ocean, refugees fled to safety and to escape the abject poverty left behind by those wars. This porous corridor still draws people north. Since 1980, using the Usumacinta River as a major route, an estimated 3.5 million Central American migrants have made it to the United States, for many, after enduring hardship and peril—rapes, beatings, robberies, murder-by-example. It's all about business, mostly the illegal kind. Everyone gets a cut, no matter how brutal or banal or indirect, from Chiapas to households in suburban Kansas City, to the restaurant owner in Chicago, to the painting contractor in Boston. As one Guatemalan told me when I asked why his people take the risk to immigrate to America, he said, with more than a little sarcasm, "They can't afford a ticket to Norway [with the highest per capita income in the world], so they go to the U.S."

At the Guatemala border, Mexicans appear to have the same patronizing attitude toward impoverished Central Americans as Americans evidently have toward Mexicans. Migrants arrive here homesick with few belongings and the phone number of an uncle, cousin or family contact. Some pay "coyotes" thousands of dollars for transport all the way to the U.S. border; others do it the only way they can, on the cheap. Here in eastern Chiapas the assault rate is high. Banditos and bribe-happy officials lurk along the river transit points preying on migrants. They are no less opportunistic than the fish hawks circling the blue skies above.

❂ ❂ ❂

The river looped wide into a horseshoe bend. At the top of the shoe, through a canopy of hardwoods, a bank of lichen-covered limestone gave away the Maya river redoubt of Yaxchilan. Following the path of the ancients, we debarked and climbed forest-covered stairs. From there the path wound through a twilit labyrinth of carved lintels and V-shaped corbel arches and vaults, for which Yaxchilan and the pre-classic Maya world are famous.

Sweeping down off one of those arches, a sac-winged bat swiped my neck and shoulder. At first glance Cowboy suggested that the big-eared harasser looked more like a fat, ugly butterfly. Nothing silky-winged about the harasser, though. Cowboy soon got the same treatment, "batted" across his new wide-brimmed straw hat. Yikes, they were a colony, it became apparent, a high-pitched chirping and whirring squadron of bats.

Minutes later, Cowboy and I paused beneath what was said to be 500-year-old ceiba tree. Standing in a mulch of leaf cutter ants and the scat of howler monkeys, we could hear shrieking and brachiating from the canopy tops near the royal acropolis. The rotund boatman, walking with the aid of a fresh-cut cane and still catching his breath from the climb, explained in Spanish to a couple from Oaxaca, and to me in broken English, that the ceiba was the Maya universe stratified (or the "World Tree"), rooting in the underworld, shooting up through the terrestrial realm and towering beyond to the heavenly canopies. The ancients, the boatman said, could climb the ceiba as swiftly as a howler monkey.

Through the palisade of trees fronting the river I could hear the hum of passing jon boats and see their dithering shadows. We stood before the primly-clipped Great Plaza, once the scene of grand public ceremonies and now scattered with the tumbled stones of palaces and

82

temples, with lintels, steles and statues depicting jaguars, crocodiles, queens and kings with names like Bird Jaguar and Shield Jaguar. And all Maya and pre-Columbian cities had ball courts, as common then as soccer fields are in local villages today. For the ancients, the *pelota* games were played as ritual war (like the Red Sox and Yankees).

As a symbol of divine sacrifice, bloodletting was a common practice at Yaxchilan. Our boatman drew his cane across the incisions of one lintel that depicted Lady Xoc pulling a rope through her tongue, while Shield Jaguar, her husband, wearing a "drum major headdress," held the torch. Unlike Cambodia's Hindu imagery at Angkor, none of the Maya monuments glorified sex; propitiating the gods was paramount.

More often than not it was the men, if not the king, using an obsidian blade or stingray spine to cut their tongue or penis, returning blood to the gods who had given their own to create the Maya. The ritualized practice was performed for every purpose from maintaining the social-political balance of the universe to the more mundane blessing of births, weddings and new buildings. Known as *kulel*, or soul force, in this way all Maya buildings are anointed with the spirit of life, for gods and humans alike. Even today, Maya dedicate their homes with a live offering by sacrificing a goat or a chicken.

Following the fierce cry of the black howlers, we climbed the steep hillside to a well-preserved temple built by Bird Jaguar IV. Light filtered through the canopy, and with a few bounding branches to train our eyes on, we watched the howlers swing and hang along their arboreal byways, feeding on fruits and nuts and leaves. Fronting the temple is a bas relief of a ball game, and inside is a statue of Bird Jaguar, its head lost to the Tabasco timber merchants.

As demand for the illegal cutting of the Lacandon timber—mahogany, Cristobal, Santa Maria, cabbage bark, and other specialty woods—continues unabated, logging roads now web the riparian forests. Timber merchants cross the river into Guatemala's Sierra del

Lacandon each year, felling tens of thousands of tropical woods. The few remaining forest-dwelling Lacandones are slowly being coaxed into villages by evangelical missionaries; those who remain are understandably drawn to the rewards of cutting old growth forest. One conservationist called the deforestation here, estimated at ninety percent, a "supermarket without a checkout counter."

Like the fate of the Khmers who built Angkor, down the La Ruta Maya, from Palenque and Yaxchilan to Tikal and on east to Copan in Honduras, some mix of war, famine, drought, overpopulation, and environmental degradation brought an end to the Maya empire. Both Khmer and Maya empires existed as parallel universes a millennium ago, but have long since failed to revisit their days of grandeur; they are now among the poorest regions in the world. Might the history of the Khmers and Maya remind us of where human arrogance toward the environment will lead?

As we returned to the Usumacinta, the boatman told us the politicians back in Mexico City and Guatemala City wanted to dam the river, Yucatan's most important trade route for centuries. In an open letter to Mexico's president, local Maya expressed their concern for the environment and reminded all Americans of the shared gift from our pre-Columbian past: "The Usumacinta is more than just the water in the channel. It is the lifeblood of Mesoamerica, and one of the birthplaces of culture and meaning in the Western Hemisphere. Historically, it will outlast whatever less durable and transcendent projects humans may devise." Between the Zapatistas and the Guatemalan Maya, whose ancient home is along the river, the likelihood of a dam not being blown to smithereens is almost nada.

❂ ❂ ❂

Tanagers, scarlet macaws, and keel-bill toucans crisscrossed the Great Plaza at Bonampak, a Maya tributary city of Yaxchilan only a few miles upriver. Clouds of hummingbirds glittered like emeralds at the forest edge which throbbed with the sweet throatings of friendly birds. Until a local Maya showed Giles Healey, an American explorer and photographer, the ruins of Bonampak in 1946, no outsiders knew of its existence. Upon Healey's arrival, recently-burned copal (natural incense) would have perfumed the ancient altars, then overtaken by vegetative rage.

Healey must have been doubly astonished at his discovery that Maya, theretofore believed to have been unwarlike, gentle agrarians, were far from peaceable. The tranquil images found on their pottery were a far remove from Bonampak's masterpiece frescoes that tell the story of a dynamic battle with hand-to-hand combat and gouging spears. In one scene warrior king Chan Muwan II, nephew of Yaxchilan's Shield Jaguar, steadies a thrusting spear adorned in jaguar pelts. As the victor, the jaguar-skin-clad king oversees fingernail-bloodletting of the captives (who were most likely sacrificed). In the modest Templo de las Pinturas, hieroglyphics provide all the names, occupations and dates, recorded with the same systematic rigor of a modern-day police blotter and the triumphal propagandizing of a king.

❂ ❂ ❂

An hour later, as the sun was falling, Cowboy and I climbed the pyramidal base to a copper-colored, lichen-covered temple. Joining us was an American gay couple we had met on the boat—Robert, a novelist, Vietnam vet, Spanish-speaking Maya aficionado and literature professor at a liberal arts college in Ohio, and Ted, a successful sculptor in his mid-seventies. Though we got along well with Robert and Ted, Cowboy and I had buffooned our introductions to them, me by asking Robert if Ted was his dad, and Cowboy by telling Ted that he reminded him of George Washington (and he did have that stature). The lug headiness got worse: When Cowboy found out Robert came of age in Weatherford, Texas, he talked up a whorehouse he had visited there in his rodeo days, almost forty years before. Bemused fails to explain Robert's and Ted's expressions.

In step, we walked beyond the plaza, taking in the view of the yellow-daubed forest canopy of the Usumacinta river valley. In the thin upper branches of a slick-barked "Palomulatto" tree (as the park cop called it), dozens of the colorfully-plumaged tropical orioles (Montezuma oropendolas), chestnut with bright yellow tails and red beaks, performed a mating ritual. First "bowing," then making a full trapeze spin, all the time gurgling and sounding a loud crackling call. Furiously, the female birds—smaller in size but with similar plumage—came and went from the forest, all the time patching and pasting together their hanging-sausage-like nests. Silky-winged monarch butterflies flitted by during the ritual, spreading their tiger-colors like sails and vanished swiftly.

Cowboy and I wanted to see more ruins, but other than the 200-square-mile forest around Tikal, there would be nothing so spectacular as the Lacandon jungle until the rain forests of Costa Rica. Fuel, food, timber and exotic game demands have taken their toll throughout most Central American forests.

"You could throw a cat through the cracks in my room," Cowboy said, complaining of the shoddy sawn planking of the Maya family's guest hut we rented near the river. Staying there felt like the bittersweet rhythms of tropical camping: frogs croaking, bats whirring, and cicada buzzing late into the night. We sprayed down, but still had to swat mosquitoes while centipedes and hairy spiders spackled the ceiling and giant moths hovered around a solitary bulb. In the pre-dawn glow, the birdsong began and played until shafts of sunlight fell through the cat-wide cracks. It was then I noticed the blond hair and big brown eyes of a young boy, curiously staring in on me as I sat up reading. The biracial ten-year-old, fathered by a German traveler who apparently kept on going, had been sent by his mother to turn on a broken hot water heater. By the time I unlatched the door, the kid, frightened, ran away.

The early sunrise washed the sluggish brown river in a brassy shade. In the open-air, stand-alone kitchen next to our hut, a twenty-something senora was cooking us a hardy breakfast of sunny-side-up eggs, a comal pan of corn tortillas and a pot of refried beans before we made tracks to the border crossing. Fearful of catching a stray microbe, Cowboy cautiously downed the eggs and tortillas and poked at the beans while mumbling some country pearl about picking fly shit out of the pepper.

Twenty minutes after that tasty repast we were at the sleepy Frontera Corozal customs station, first in line that morning to get stamped out of Mexico (and perhaps into Guatemala). The cruel-faced, chubby official manning the immigration window thumbed my passport first. "This is a problem," he said, scowling, feigning concern over my lack of an entry stamp to Mexico (remember: back in Laredo). As I paid him the departure tax, I asked what I could do to make the problem disappear. He gave me the ol' studied silence look, perfected with thousands of passersby before me. Then shazam, *mordida*, the bribe, a couple of Abe Lincolns fell freely out of my hand onto his desk. Cowboy followed suit. Problem solved: He stamped us out, tucked the bills in his pocket and waved us toward the river.

Benjamin, a cocky thirty-something Mexican Fokker pilot with Air Mexico, who was touring Maya ruins from here to Copan, sat across from me on the thatch-covered jon boat. Next to him was a Spanish couple from Barcelona; he a government economist, both in their early thirties. "Why are you guys not at the beach in Cancun, eating at McDonald's?" Benjamin asked Cowboy and me, half-joking but mocking the odd American found off the beaten path.

"Been there," Cowboy shot back. "Why, do you think Americans have a problem with Mexico?"

"They are not interested in our culture," Benjamin said. "They bring their own. When I was in India I didn't ask for enchiladas."

Though I got his point, I wondered to myself why there was, thankfully, a taqueria on damned near every corner in my home base, Cambridge, Mass.

At the same time, the Spanish couple had been engaging. Curious about Cortes' place in his country's history, I asked how he was presented in schools back in Spain.

"We studied about *colons* and the wealth that Spain enjoyed, but nothing serious about Cortes," the Spanish economist said. "When I first came to Mexico three years ago I learned about Cortes's conquests in the New World." It sounded familiar: white-washing history, Columbus discovering America, the heroic U.S. conquest of Mexico and all that.

There was more small talk, before I asked a brooding Benjamin what he thought of NAFTA.

"It's bad for farmers and small business."

"What about the jobs?"

"That's good but the profits go back to the States," he said, holding his hands up and open as if to add, tell me it's not true. As was his nature, he grasped only one side of the story, leaving out the dire impacts on American factory workers and their hometowns.

❂ ❂ ❂

A knot of moneychangers awaited us on the river's eastern shores in Guatemala. They were hustlin' biz with an odd assortment of young backpackers, a single Japanese man, and Dutch, German, Danish and Argentine couples, all speaking some, if not fluent, Spanish. Conspicuously absent among the worldly-wise swarm of tumbleweeds were American youth. These blowin-in-the-wind types had spent the night in Bethel, Guatemala, a scrofulous assortment of sawn-plank huts and run-down buses near the boat dock, waiting for the first ride out this morning. Paying ten bucks a piece, we loaded on to a smallish, twenty-passenger bus for the hot and dusty, five-hour ride to Flores. The driver's handy-man assistant had me move aside while he opened the battery cover and jiggered the cables as the driver turned the ignition. Several attempts later, the engine groaned to a start and a ripple of applause circled the bus.

A few miles down the road we drew up to the customs station. There, a three-foot-long caiman (small crocodile) tethered with a thin rope greeted us at the front door, with another one stationed in the back. Perhaps, without shame or disguise, the border police were signaling their complicity in the pelt and plume and live animal trade here. Thirty minutes later, passports stamped, we were bouncing along the dirt track, the route of Fire is Born, and a thousand years on, Hernando Cortes. With windows open, dust rose up in a rooster tail behind us, while fresh scenery unfolded before us. Clusters of *bajareque*, Maya peasant homes fashioned out of mud and cane poles, shared the bottom land. Banana trees lined the road, their fronds drooping like tired old flags in the tropical heat. Small plots of corn and beans spotted the landscape. A man on a motorcycle and another on a horse, both wearing white straw rancher's hats, were pulled over beneath a shade tree having a palaver. "Look at that bony horse," Cowboy exclaimed. "The guys back in Oklahoma won't believe that." Further, a small herd of well-fed zebu cattle blocked the road. Given all the clear-cutting and porous border, cattle are often brought over from Mexico to pasture.

Before the fall of the Maya Empire, as many as two million people lived in this lowland region known as El Peten, about one-third of the land in Guatemala. It is widely believed that most of those post-classical-era Maya survivors living in Peten migrated a thousand years ago to the south, to the highlands between Guatemala City and Quetzaltenango. Cortes described a few scattered Maya *aldeas*, or villages, in the dense forest. As of the late '50s there were only 26,000 living in the region, but today there are over 450,000 land-hungry campesinos. Mexican loggers in cahoots with Guatemalan army officers have stripped much of El Peten's old-growth forests of their mahogany and other hardwoods, making way for excessive home-steading, cattle ranching, and maize farming. It's rapidly changing into a dust bowl of hardscrabble farms.

Never far away was a brightly painted *tienda*, a small store with snacks, soap, chickens, watermelon and drinks, and nearby, almost always, was a one-room evangelical or Pentecostal church. In a country once overwhelmingly synonymous with the rites and rituals of Catholicism, up to forty percent of Guatemalans are now Protestant, a trend that began in the 1980s. Although Maya are close to a majority in Guatemala, *"ladinos,"* a mix of Maya and European, make up the ruling class here. Their dominance has been a 400-year-old source of tension. Throwing more fuel on the fire are the strained relations between evangelicals and Catholics (like Sunnis and Shias in the Middle East).

❂ ❂ ❂

In the '80s, perceiving the widespread adoption of liberation theology south of the border as Marxist, the Reagan administration reached out to Latin American dictators and evangelical groups, some say with the furor of a crusade, to oppose this push for social change. By 1987, Chile's dictator Augusto Pinochet and El Salvador's military government hosted Jimmy Swaggart, Louisiana's finest anti-Catholic, evangelical preacher; he packed sports' stadiums in the two countries.

In Guatemala, dictator and President Efrain Rios Montt was so enraged at the Catholic Church's criticism of the military's bloodlet-ting that he converted to fundamentalist religion and became a hell-fire-ranting minister in the California-based Gospel Church of the Word. And there's no wrath like the scorched earth rage of a new-born renunciate. In Montt's sham-godly version of the evangelical movement, every Maya man, woman and child became a potential subversive suspect. Given that, he deployed the ladino military to decimate rural campesino villages.

90

This period became known as *la escoba*, or the broom, when violence swept the country. Possessed with a proselytizing fervor, evangelical preachers called the guerillas the devil, and the officer class of the military spread the word that all Catholic priests were communists. It was a feudalistic savagery driven by a shared mythology and a mutual hate—rich against poor, light skin ladinos against dark skin Indians, natives against immigrants, Protestant against Catholic, the U.S. against the Soviet Union. The Guatemalan army concocted a "pacification" program (similar to one the U.S. imposed in South Vietnam). Spearheaded and encouraged by the million-man Civil Defense Patrols, villagers spied on, tortured and killed other villagers. Hard-core guerillas, whose numbers were less than 10,000, assassinated random patrons and politicians. The government army massacred peasants with a fury. By one estimate the ratio of killings carried out by the government to those by guerillas was 100 to one. It was institutionalized terrorism and not the more banal thrust and parry of Cold War ideas.

In 1951, the democratic election of Colonel Jacobo Arbenz was only the second in Guatemalan history. The country had been ruled for almost a century by dictators controlled by the military and coffee interests. These despots were mostly of European ethnicity—New World Spaniards (*criollos*) and Germans. Wasting no time, President Arbenz, a socialist, embraced the reforms of his clement predecessor, Juan Jose Arevalao, who allowed unions, mandated an eight-hour work day, outlawed forced labor and the paltry wages that began with the Spanish Conquest, and set upon a course of agrarian reform. The plan was for the government to purchase, at values submitted for tax assessments, the "uncultivated" land of the sugar, banana, cotton and coffee *fincas* and the cattle ranches, and redistribute it on a tenancy basis to almost half a million Maya (the hereditary owners).

The American Homestead Act was the model for Arbenz's Decree 900, the 1952 "Law of Agrarian Reform," which, it is said, was intended to have Maya become Lincoln's "yeoman farmers," to "overcome the economic backwardness" of the country and "improve the quality of life of the masses." In a Cold War context, however, all that reform rigmarole read as code for pinko. Guatemalan Communist Party members did indeed advise Arbenz, but at its core Decree 900 reinforced private ownership of property, for patrons and peasants alike.

Arriving in Guatemala during the Arbenz years was a twenty-five-year-old Argentine physician and would-be revolutionary, Ernesto Guevara, who would later become known by his nickname, Che. He was there trying to sort out what he could do to address Latin America's social ills. According to Daniel Wilkinson in *Silence on the Mountain*, Che got his answer watching the 1954 CIA-sponsored coup d'état that deposed the democratically elected President Jacobo Arbenz: Make war against U.S. imperialism.

The coup was one of the darkest pages in U.S. relations with Latin America, plunging Guatemala into over three decades of war, lawlessness and despair. As it happened, the Yankee intelligence agency was just coming into its own. In Iran, only months before, a CIA coup d'état had brazenly toppled the democratically-elected Prime Minister Mohammed Mossadegh, and replaced him with the American-friendly shah.

At the time, the American-based United Fruit Company (now Chiquita Brands International) was the largest landowner in Guatemala, controlling eighty-five percent of the country's uncultivated land. United Fruit's stockholders included Secretary of State John Foster Dulles, his brother CIA director Allen Dulles, and undersecretary of State Walter Bedell Smith. United Fruit was already well-known in Latin America for the "Banana Massacre," which occurred in 1928 at a plant in Santa Marta, Colombia. In that assault on democracy, as many as 2,000 banana union protesters were killed by Colombian government troops, with the full force of American State Department backing. Venezuelan Nobel laureate Gabriel Garcia Marquez's '60s novel, *One Hundred Years of Solitude*, rekindled the memory of the 1928 tragedy.

On June 18, 1954, led by two Guatemalan army officers, the CIA launched an invasion of Guatemala from Honduras, and U.S. newspapers went along with the CIA narrative that Guatemalans had organized the operation. American Ambassador John Peurifoy famously stood atop the embassy in Guatemala City and directed bombing raids by mercenaries who had been dispatched by Allen Dulles' CIA. The Guatemalan military was no match for what the U.S. would throw at them and folded before ever engaging. Ending a decade of democracy, President Arbenz resigned and took asylum in the Mexico embassy. Before leaving the country the CIA-hand-picked junta leader Colonel Carlos Castillo, a consummate army man, forced Arbenz to strip to his underwear at the airport in front of a crowd of American surrogates.

After his ousting and public humiliation, President Arbenz was a broken man; he died in Mexico years later at age fifty-eight under mysterious circumstances. In America, President Eisenhower, proclaimed the junta "a showcase for democracy." In a matter of weeks, a decade of reform in Guatemala had been undone. Years later, an exhaustive CIA investigation into Guatemala's alleged Soviet connection, including an analysis of over 150,000 documents, turned up nothing.

In the late '90s, according to Guatemala's Truth Commission report, the thirty-six-year civil war that followed that CIA coup left over 200,000 dead and a million homeless, forced off the uncultivated lands of the plantations. Thousands more just disappeared. Today, over a third of the country lives below the poverty line, and by all indices of life expectancy, education, literacy and GDP, Guatemala is among the lowest in the world. One in ten, or over a million, Guatemalans (mostly Maya) fled to camps in Mexico and then to the U.S. As of

2023, remittances home from Guatemalan emigrants to the U.S. accounts for twenty percent of the country's GDP.

✿ ✿ ✿

El Peten didn't get its first paved road until 1982, which may explain why we didn't hit asphalt on our five-hour bus ride until twenty miles out of Flores. By that time, our tired old bus had developed a noticeable wobble. The handyman assistant told us that one of the dually rear tires was "broken," but with no spare, the driver was pushing on. Swerving as if drunk from ditch to ditch, the assistant hung out the side door, eyeing the depleted tire as if waiting for it to fall off so he could signal the driver to stop. We mercifully limped into Santa Elena late in the afternoon, slightly punch drunk from the unsteady ride, skin pores, clothes and rucksacks covered with the dust of the road.

We caught a tuk-tuk (rotativo) in Santa Elena across the causeway to Flores, encircled by Lake Peten Itza, meaning "enchanted waters." While en route to Honduras, Cortes had arrived here in 1524, when Flores was known as Tayasal. His visit was improbably peaceful, and he left behind one of his horses, an animal the Maya Itza had never seen before. They later made a stone effigy of the horse, which they worshiped as the "thunder tapir." Otherwise the Maya Itza, a war-like tribe, weren't so welcoming: It would be another 150 years before Tayasal, the only remaining independent Maya city, fell to Spanish rule. During the final conquest, all pyramids and temples were destroyed, replaced by the cathedral atop the hill near where we were staying.

Still thinking about his mules in Colorado and his new cabin there with empty walls, Cowboy spent the evening going from shop to shop inquiring about "mule art," with no luck. After a restful night's sleep in a posada on the lake, we caught a colectivo for the hour's ride to Tikal, the great Maya jungle city-state where Fire is Born settled a millennium and a half before. That morning Cowboy broke out the camouflage, a wide-brimmed hat, scarf, cargo pants, backpack, accented by a shocking pink, long-sleeve tee-shirt. Commandant Cowboy meets Barbie, the last word on south-of-the-border bus riding fashion?

As we circled the lake, painted rocks and posters on utility poles advertised the coming election, with seventeen candidates competing. "Rigoberta Menchu is running for president," said Felipe, the Indian driver/guide, invoking the name of the Nobel Laureate who lost her parents, two brothers, a sister-in-law and three nieces and nephews during the civil war. "She may be the first Mayan head of state here since before the Spanish arrived."

"Does she have a chance to win?" I shouted above the din from the back seat.

"Maybe, but it doesn't matter. We [Mayans] have no choice but to vote for her."

As it turned out, the whirligigs of time did not come her way; she received a paltry three percent of the vote.

On several occasions, I tried to strike up a conversation with Felipe about the war, but getting someone to talk about the violence here reminded me of the war-fatigued Burmese when I asked similar questions. The response was always the same: recoil and a gaze around the room, "eyes deep in hell," before saying, "the walls talk." But here in Guatemala they say, *"A saber,"* or, "Who knows?"

Felipe did, however, talk about Guatemala as a kind of South Africa of the Americas, with a feudalistic, apartheid system that favors ladinos. "Twenty percent of Mayans here don't speak Spanish," he told us. "They were made to go to the Catholic Church, but the priests spoke Latin. So, they didn't learn; they are still illiterate."

As we approached the Tikal National Park, several ocellated turkeys, flashing in iridescent blue, scratched their way down the road. Above, in the canopy, the driver pointed out a brace of toucans. Nearby, the branches of a ceiba were filled with the colorful orioles, bowing and spinning in their mating ritual. Further along, the park was crawling with fatigued soldiers carrying automatic weapons. President Oscar Berger's daughter was visiting.

A small group of day-tripping Mormons, who had arrived on the early flight from Guatemala City, and would be returning there at five, gathered by the park's lagoon for a walking lecture. As a fly in the forest I caught their guide's reference to the *Book of Mormon*, which he then connected to, with a certain mythical symmetry, the Lost Tribes of Israel, Joseph Smith, and the Maya.

Standing among a throng of idle guides near the Mormons, one by one I overheard snickers, followed by sawmill whispers of "Hey Rambo, hey Rambo." Here in this Latin American, camouguerilla-revolutionary-haven, they were having fun with Cowboy's choice of clothes. Felipe, our guide, joined in, "He should go kidnap Chavez for the CIA."

The organic mystique of Tikal would be lost if not for Peten's steamy, subtropical rain forest: the green heart of the Maya world that aggressively bays like a protective dog at the ancient city's edges. As with most days, the rain forest was hot and churning out undulating clouds of vapors, a blue floating mist. As we watched several raccoon-like coatimundi sniffing the ground for insects, the forest came alive, throbbing with the shrieks of parrots flashing by, the squawks of toucans, the screeching calls of howlers and the cracking swoosh of canopy branches bending and swaying with spread-eagling spider monkeys. Strangler figs, snake-like lianas and creepers crisscrossed the canopy and colorful bursts of blooming epiphytes—the flowers of the air—grew out of moss-like nests.

Felipe stopped along the path to show us a sapodilla tree whose milky sap, known as *chicle*, was once used as the base in our Chiclets and Wrigley's Spearmint gum and has now been replaced by an oil-based synthetic. *Chicleros*, a dying breed of forest cowboys, still harvest and sell the chicle even while sapodillas are disappearing from overuse. Farther along, Felipe plucked cilantro from the ground cover, passing it around, and then had us sniff the fruit and leaves of the allspice bush, which smelled strongly of clove and is widely used for cooking. While he talked, tree frogs buzzed around us, the dead air a pungent aroma of tropical mulch and fresh bloom.

Over 100,000 people once lived in the twenty-three square miles of the religious, commercial and cultural stronghold of Tikal, about three times the size of ancient Rome. And like the Eternal City, the resource demands of constant war and the extravagant indulgences of Tikal's kings and courtiers idling, drinking *kusha*, a moonshine concoction of fermented fruit, and sipping spicy chocolate, signaled their end. The lower classes, Felipe said, lived among the tropical cedars and mahoganies in perishable huts made of wood and mud. They were obligated to give 100 days of labor each year. Yet, he was quick to say, they weren't slaves, but rather artisans and maize farmers paying tribute for protection.

The middle-class Maya, he continued, were warriors, once led by Lord Chocolate and known for their stealth in surrounding enemy armies before skillfully hurling obsidian-tipped spears at these foes. Captured armies became assets, more stonemasons and sculptors for building temples and palaces. Vassal states also paid tribute in labor and trade goods, jade, bird plumes, cacao beans, and obsidian.

And again, culture follows power, about as seamlessly in hindsight as changing sets at on a Broadway play. As the ruling class of priests and demigods who lived in the acropolis prospered, they championed new construction of temples, pyramids, plazas, and urban public works systems. To support the nobility, the Maya practiced intensive agriculture in what are now abandoned swamps. "A network of canals and raised fields (similar to the Aztec floating gardens) allowed large populations to thrive in the jungle, an achievement equaled only by the Khmer of Cambodia somewhat later," wrote Ronald Wright in *Stolen Continents*. Those canals, which were once stocked with fish, still trace Tikal's many causeways.

Felipe led us up a man-made hilltop, past True-Great-Jaguar-Claw's palace, tracking a steep pathway around a lichen-covered temple. Soon we breasted a panoramic point that looked upon Tikal's Great Plaza, its sublime architectural splendor redolent of Fire is Born's native city-state of Teotihuacan. Tikal means "place of voices," explaining why shamans once climbed to the pyramid tops to talk. The settlement of Tikal goes back to 900 B.C.—the time of Solomon's temple—but what is seen today was produced in the Maya classical period: the oldest stele here was erected in 292 A.D. in the time of Foliated Jaguar.

To the east, the extraordinary nine-story, 150-foot jaguar temple, tomb of Jasaw Chan K'awiil I, faced off with the 125-foot Moon temple, tomb of his wife Lady Twelve Macaw. The grandeur, like skyscrapers piercing the canopy as symbols of power and custom, struck me as a Stone Age version of the Petronas Towers in Kuala Lumpur (once the world's tallest). Unlike modern towers, which are crowned with a mundane spindle and will not be around in 1,500 years, Tikal's ancient temples are crested by a chambered platform with a roof comb, once gloriously washed in red cinnabar.

Straight ahead, stele, altars, patios, palaces, tombs, bas-relief and palaces, layered and accreted like a geologist's stratigraphic map, advanced up the northern end of the plaza, forming the central acropolis. Hieroglyphics fill in some of the blanks with timelines of war, gods, kings and commerce, but had it not been for the purge-the-devil bonfire of hundreds of Maya books and codices by Yucatan Bishop Diego de Landa in 1562, we would all be better informed.

Ritual ceremony—communicating with the dead, drawing blood from the tongue and penis, dancing to a drum beat and trancing out on hallucinogenic plant drugs—was held around the Irish-green swath in the plaza. In 1996, Felipe said, the Maya were allowed to return to Tikal to worship, to burn incense on the Day of the Dead and to heal the sick. There is now a modern, Anti-Columbus

Day festival, reported the *New York Times*, to show Americans and Europeans that after almost five centuries of imperialism, the Maya Indians are still practicing the old ways.

> Father Sun, Mother Moon, Father Wind, Mother Earth, the head shaman cried in Quiche, starting the prayer. ...The shaman bowed to the ground, his necklace of jade and shells rattling, and the hundreds of gathered Mayans did likewise. His voice fell, the public prayer becoming a private one, and a chorus of chattering voices rose to join him. Guatemala has 22 dialects, and these people were speaking in all of them, asking their ancient gods for help, for health, for money and friendship. ...The shamans—there were four or five altogether—piled candles, eggs, incense, sage, tobacco, leaves and rum in a large stone pit and lighted it. Flames leapt 20 feet in the air, and the people danced in clove-scented smoke, circling to the clunky beat of the marimba.

The Passion and Protesting Bush

Chapter Four

IT'S AN URBAN MYTH that old American school buses die and go to the junkyard. In fact, they go to Guatemala and get a makeover, with added chrome plating, primary colors and an optional plastic Jesus. They are reborn as third-class "Chicken buses," so named for their barnyard cargo, and for the open seating atop the roof.

It was nine at night as we stretched across our bags on the porch of the Casa Blanca. Joining us were two early-twenties American girls, both skimpily clad, fresh off a bus from Belize City (where we'd also spent a couple of uneventful nights). The red-headed one was hoarse from an all-night drinking adventure. Apparently, they had endured a long day. "Get me back to America," said the redheaded one, while the other pitched in with a honey-dipped accent, "If only I saw a sign that said, 'Florida, next stop.'"

On time, our 70s model, two-toned green school bus drew up and honked. The overnighter to Guatemala City had arrived, and to our surprise, it had air conditioning. The bus was already packed with locals, luggage and crates, and tightly sealed with cheesy, forest green curtains, better for sleep. Cowboy took the only empty seat in the front and wrapped his neck in his first-class pillow, while I grabbed the only other seat, on the aisle in the middle of the bus. The man occupying the seat next to me was like a corpse, lifeless but for the occasional nasal wheeze. Besotted as well, the fumes told me. Decorously, from across the aisle a nicely dressed man greeted me

100

with a capacious smile. Within minutes, he told me that he was an obstetrician-gynecologist in Santa Elena, which shouldn't have been a surprise. Everyone on the bus seemed to know him and his wife, who I soon learned was his office manager.

Cautiously, the way I suspect guerilla insurgents might suss out a stranger, I told him that my wife worked with many ob-gyns in Africa and Asia. Instantly, he got the code, leaning across the aisle, beaming with mischief.

"I work with Planned Parenthood of Alabama," he told me, with his hand cupped around his mouth as if the corpse next to me might be listening. "Their doctors and clinicians come here some of the time, and I have been there once. My wife and I like doing family planning."

We were safe to talk, just not too loud. When I told him that my wife had been head of Planned Parenthood's Africa division, we discussed the population explosion, poverty and the religious politics that drive it. "If missionaries want to come here and build schools and hospitals, let them come. But they shouldn't be telling people what to do with their lives," he told me while yawning. I never found out if he was Catholic, evangelical, Maya or indifferent. A few minutes later, he was curled around his wife, sleeping, as was the rest of the bus.

❂ ❂ ❂

Oddly enough, the day before I had met a group of do-gooders who almost fit the doc's development model. Having lunch in the Tikal forest was a day-tripping gathering of American Orthodox Christians on a church mission. As their story went, in 1857 Hogar Rafael Ayau built the first orphanage in Guatemala City. These Orthodox of Russian, Carpathian and Greek descent were there to build a new Hogar Rafael Ayau Orphanage, but away from Guatemala City's crime-ravaged downtown. "Kids should not have to grow up around gangs, gunshots, prostitutes and transvestites," the thirty-something social worker named Danny from San Francisco told me. Kitted out in a Jungle Jim outfit of new khaki everything, he continued, "The problem is that the Jesuits own the land and now they have cut off the water. After meeting those kids, we will go back and get the church to fund a new location as fast as possible."

Though not indifferent to the toll taken by war or the unique circumstances that had turned those kids into orphans, I told Danny that with more family planning (for example, the rhythm method, IUDs, the pill), there would be less poverty and fewer orphans. Having never been to a Third World peasant village, he hewed to a more doctrinaire, less pragmatic cast of mind: "Fertilizing the egg is the criteria for us. Condoms are okay but not the pill." Danny then referred me to 1st Corinthians and Paul's condemnation of sexual immorality for more modern-day guidance on the birds and the bees.

After the earthquake of 1976, which killed 27,000, injured 75,000 and left a million homeless in the Maya highlands, refugees flooded into Guatemala City (also known as Guat); they were followed by evangelical emergency relief missions from the U.S. Neither group ever left Guat. With the civil war raging, evangelicals, assisted by the Catholics-are-communists Reagan Doctrine a few years later, found a willing audience of both Maya and ladinos. The Protestant message of "individual enterprise, puritanical temperance, and redemption through prayer," resonated. And, with the blood of the civil war and earthquake fresh, so did their apocalyptic prophecy. Almost overnight, Guat mushroomed from 650,000 people to a population in the metropolitan area of over four million. Today, it's the largest city in Central America. As Danny told me, "It's not a city for kids to grow up in, the Sugar Plum Fairy has left the house." Nor is it a place for wandering travelers. Government warnings about Guat's grinding poverty and slums, drug and street gangs, kidnappings and death squads, advise foreigners to keep on moving.

We broached the outskirts of the capital city at four-thirty in the morning. With the crush of traffic, it was seven before we got to the bus station. Only two weeks before, three Salvadoran legislators, traveling to Guat by caravan with a police escort for a meeting of the Central America Parliament, had been kidnapped, tortured, murdered and torched. While officials said a Mexican drug operation was behind it, four Guatemalan police officers had been arrested and placed in a maximum-security facility. The officers had been tracked to the scene of the murder by their cell phone signals. One of the victims was Eduardo Jose D'Aubuisson, son of the founder of El Salvador's ruling party. Amid the hue and cry from San Salvador and the international human rights community, Guatemalan President Oscar Berger called in the FBI.

Before the FBI could get there to interview the police officers, who had admitted their guilt but had not identified their accomplices, a brazen gang of masked men with AK-47s were given entrance access to the prison and gunned down the four policemen. So, who killed the killers, the only witnesses? That no high-level arrests have been made should be an embarrassment to the Guatemalan government. All fingers seem to point at a shadow group of evangelical, retired military officers known as "La Cofradia," or the Brotherhood. Although their motives are unclear, it is safe to say that wars and genocide rarely have tidy endings.

❂ ❂ ❂

It looked like a red alert had been signaled in the downtown neighborhood of Guat. Soldiers and riot police were on every corner or behind concrete barricades with automatic weapons. Banners written in red attacking *yanquis* draped the buildings and barricades. President George W. Bush was arriving in two days, and with the murders of the Salvadorans still fresh, security was not being left to chance. Cowboy and I grabbed the first colectivo and vamoosed to the 16th century Spanish capital of Antigua (nee Santiago), a forty-five-minute drive.

Winding down into the Valley of Panchoy, the patched and rusted minibus seemed to shake off parts as we jounced wildly along the cobblestone streets of Antigua's central plaza, past the mermaid fountain and the gothic Santiago Cathedral, the stately, colonnaded Captain-Generals' Palace and a long arcade of shops. A line of sullen-faced men in straw hats, coffee plantation migrants, twisted around the square from the bank next door to the palace, each there to give a thumb print to cash their weekly checks.

Beyond the plaza, the low-slung city, built to withstand earth-quakes, broke away in a grid, bursting alive with pastel-painted stucco homes, four to a block. Each house was fitted with large wooden doors for entryways (*zaguans*) adorned with high-set brass knockers, once used by horsemen so as not to have to dismount to enter. Behind those doors were courtyards and patios, bedecked in gar-goyles and fountains and tropical lush, surrounded by rooms for all uses and stables in the back. Three volcanoes, Fuego, Acatenago and Aqua, rise above Antigua, at once portentous and picture-perfect, on this day with wisps of white hanging above each peak like curlicues exclaiming their magnificence.

❂ ❂ ❂

A ladino Catholic town of 14,000, Antigua once ruled over Spanish lands from Chiapas to El Salvador, Nicaragua and Costa Rica. The city's past and present are freighted with the calamities of colonial history and natural disasters. Dispatched here by Cortes in 1524, Pedro de Alvarado's army mercilessly conquered the Maya highlands, murdering tens of thousands. European diseases—small-pox, yellow fever, influenza and more—spread in the wake of Alvarado's army and later Spanish settlement, further decimating Maya villages. Repeated earthquakes in Ciudad Vieja forced the Spanish to move their capital to Antigua, while more of the same compelled its relocation, in 1775, to Guatemala City (whose history of settlement goes back 9,000 years).

Today the living history that fills Antigua's streets draws back-packers, tourists, Spanish language students, and aid workers from everywhere. There are over 120 hotels and 100-plus restaurants here, with as many Spanish immersion schools and 200 weddings on any given weekend, particularly during Lent. Americans, like the ones I met day-tripping to Tikal, come here in droves to learn Spanish, to adopt babies and to do mission work with one of the 1,500 NGOs, mostly faith-based, who work in Guatemala. "But they never share what they do," Thomas Schafer Cox, a fourth-generation German gallery owner, told me. "The big projects never work. Less is more, with some Dutch lady watching over every quetzal. That works."

In the '60s and '70s American hippies arrived in Antigua in bus-load numbers. Most of those who remain, from places like Mendocino, San Francisco, New York and Minnesota, have moved on to San Marcos or Panajachel on Lake Atitlan. Today, dour, pasty-skinned southern women with floppy sun hats and sun dresses push strollers in the park with their new, bronze-colored Maya babies, as horse-drawn buggies ferry tourists around.

A constant presence on the streets is Elizabeth Bell, a fiftyish something American expatriate, who came here as a teenager with her father, and now gives architectural tours of the city. "We haven't heard yet if Bush will come to Antigua, but if he does I will be show-ing him around," she assured me when we met in front of her office. She had been President Clinton's guide for Antigua in 1999, at which time he gave an apology to Guatemala, saying that Washington "was wrong" for supporting counterinsurgency security forces.

"This is a make-up trip for Bush that means nothing," Elizabeth told me. "They will ask him for helicopters, radar and navigational equipment for their drug interdiction teams. Six years ago, he prom-ised to do something here about poverty and economic devel-opment, but then he went to Iraq. Guatemalans have been through decades of war and know what it does to the innocent. They were against the Iraq invasion from the start."

While I joined one of Elizabeth's walking tours, Cowboy blasted off on a shopping spree, buying carpets and tablecloths, three straw hats and two baseball caps, yet still no mule art. And he finally gave up his airport-friendly luggage with rollers and bought a rucksack, more suited for bus-riding. (My guess is that Cowboy's DHL bill to send all his new acquisitions to the States would have choked one of those mules he owns.)

Later that day, we took a van with Maria, a villager-cum-tour guide, and drove to San Antonio Aguas Calientes, where Maya weavers glom on to tourists like barnacles with their colorful textiles for sale. A few miles from there is the former Spanish capital of Ciudad Vieja, destroyed in a 16th century mud slide. Remnants of La Concepcion, the oldest cathedral in Guatemala, are still standing. Next door to the ruins, local Indians emerged from a Lent service that had been going on for three and a half hours, not uncommon any time of the year, Maria told us.

In the next village, San Pedro Las Huertas, enchantingly shadowed by the Fuji-like perfection of Mt. Agua, Maya women gathered in a public plaza around a pool equipped with hoses and individual wash stations for doing laundry. Across from a 16th century Spanish church at the end of the plaza, the women pay the equivalent of two dollars a year to wash every day in the public facilities. Our last stop in these Indian villages was the ladino-owned Bella Vista Farms, a coffee finca.

Thomas Schafer Cox, the gallery owner, told me that most of the fincas in Guatemala have landing strips (the Germans built many of them), often used to transship drugs from Colombia on to Mexico or the States. "A fee of $70,000 is charged for each touchdown and refueling," he said, knowingly. Hard to gage how much of this criminal intel, passed along so openly, is true.

At Bella Vista Farms, we took a slow pass around the *casa patronal*, skirted by a long veranda, before circling two warehouse-sized mills that house drying kilns and are also used for cleaning and bagging coffee. Pedro, the production superintendent, an eagle-eyed Mighty Mouse, trotted out to greet us from his office strategically located next to the loading dock and scales. From there he escorted us through the coffee fields, all shaded with chalum trees to regulate temperature, reduce water loss and improve the health of the soil. Women and their daughters, from age seven or eight to fifty, were dressed in *trajes*, traditional clothes that included a woven tunic and a wraparound skirt. Known in the industry as *limpiadoras*, or cleaners, they lined the shaded pathway, tarps spread out before them, cleaning, sorting beans for size, color (green to red), and winnowing out twigs and other trash. "They pick fifty kilos a day," Pedro said. "The children [girls] come with their mothers to help. Making money is more important than going to school."

It's true. With an average of five kids per family, a fifty-three percent illiteracy rate among Maya in the highlands, and the worst infant mortality, malnutrition, and life expectancy rates in the Western Hemisphere (Haiti excepted), the average Maya kid isn't headed for Harvard, or for that matter any college. Making up forty-four percent (some say sixty) of the population in Guatemala, Maya are slotted from day one to work on the plantations, men as supervisors and for weeding, hole digging and planting and women for picking and sorting coffee beans. Women are historically paid half as much as men, but recent studies suggest the gender gap in pay is narrowing. The training is on the job, as it has been since the industry sprang up on the piedmonts here in the 1880s with foreign capital and enterprising immigrants from Europe. From that time on, during harvest season, November to March, the Indian villages became ghost towns, emptying into the fincas. The rest of the year is called "the thin months," *los meses flacos*.

At the turn of the 20th century one-third of the coffee fincas were controlled by Germans, and the rest largely by foreign investors. The mix of ownership has changed, but the exploitation of Indigenous labor remains. Coffee is like tea: human hands are required to pick it. If it were possible to grow coffee in temperate climates, like Kansas, where poverty is not so rampant and wages are much higher, it is doubtful that consumers would pay the resulting prices. Capitalism by nature gravitates to cheap labor as witnessed in spades in Mexico's maquiladora zone (and on all the coffee plantations of Latin America).

In their zeal to make the coffee industry successful, the Guatemalan dictators of the late 19th century privatized and gave away the rich, fertile, volcanic communal land of the Maya, lush in fruit orchards and fields of beans and corn. A similar model of privatization— beggaring the Indigenes to the point of starvation as a strategy to raise a workforce—was adopted throughout the coffee growing countries of Central America. "Draft laws" were invoked in Guatemala to impress Indians as indentured laborers (as Spain had done for their gold mines and other colonial industries). The economics of those times are relatively the same today, with the exception that there are protective labor laws now in force, with a minimum wage that assumes the local standard of eighteen months a year (according to the Maya Haab calendar).

"How much do they make for each kilo?" I asked Pedro.

"Seventy-five centavos," he said, which equates to about five dollars a day, or $150 a month, but only during harvest time.

"How many hours a day do they work?"

"Ten hours, six days a week, but it's seasonal. Not all the time. And they don't work on Sunday," he explained.

We walked through the drying room and out onto the loading docks that were stacked with bags ready for shipment. Pedro pointed out the smaller bags, which weigh forty-eight kilos, and told me that they sell for about $150 (with a labor cost of five dollars). The bigger ones, seventy-five kilos, sell for $300. "Most of this," he said, with a wide smile, as he waved his hand in an arc that swept over 500-plus bags ready for shipment, "will go to Walmart." The United States is far and away the biggest consumer of coffee in the world.

A bell rang on the loading dock with the scales. Pedro's eagle-eyed supervision was needed, so we fell in behind him. The pickers, faces sunken with fatigue, were now queued up, watching every move Pedro's heavy-set assistant made as each woman loaded her bag on the scales. The assistant stepped up, with Pedro's stare fixed on the scales, and read off the weights and recorded them, one after the other. It was the end of another long, punishing day in the fields. Thirty minutes on, beneath a fuchsia sky, the lights in the valley slowly twinkled on like enchanted fireflies as we thanked Pedro and headed back towards Antigua.

On the ride back, Cowboy, who was his buoyant and business-minded self, puzzled out the profit margins of coffee. With a Grande Latte back in Boston or Boca Raton selling at Starbucks for a street value of six dollars, would coffee or cocaine be more lucrative here?

❂ ❂ ❂

A few days later, leaving Cowboy behind, I visited several of the Indian villages around Lake Atitlan, San Pedro, San Antonio, San Marcos, Panajachel and Santiago. Woven on backstrap looms, the clothes worn in each village had their own colorful style, the handiwork of the early Spanish missionaries taking Arachne's art and dividing and conquering. The *traje*, or traditional Maya clothes, vary from tasseled headdresses and patterned, indigo wraparound skirts (*cortes*) and colorful *huipils*, the tunics worn by women and fancifully embroidered with animals, birds and flowers, to men in Santiago wearing straw rancher's hats and knee-length, candy-striped *calzoncillos*, practical for fishing, and cinched with a dark sash known as a *faja*.

On a boat excursion around the 5,000-feet-high, cobalt-tinged crater, in San Antonio I found a lone adolescent girl at the Catholic church altar, both praying and keening while six dogs slept on the nearby steps. What were the young girl's prayers? Did anyone hear them? Questions that stuck in my mind.

On the opposite shore in San Marcos, where the 60s-era hippies have taken over, foreign escapists flock to learn about Hatha Yoga, traditional Jewish Kabbalah, Shaluha-ka healing treatments, channeling, oracles, and astral traveling. Pyramid-shaped cabins were set among luxuriant groves of avocado, peach, and apple trees and rows of coffee plants. In this foreigner's bubble of hippie optimism, beyond the trammels of society, at ten in the morning one woman was perched at her computer behind a cabin window with an idyllic view, writing the great American novel, I was told. Nearby in a flower garden a shirtless young blond man smoked a joint with two women, both wearing their hair in corn rows. All that was missing in this 60s-era time capsule was a tribal fire ring and a platter of Carlos Castaneda's peyote.

"Lake Como, it seems to me, touches the limit of the permissibly picturesque," wrote Aldous Huxley, in the 1930s. "But Atitlan is Como with the additional embellishment of several immense volcanoes. It really is too much of a good thing."

In San Pedro, a short boat ride away, one couldn't miss the Primera Iglesia Bautista (First Baptist Church). It looks like a cruise ship, crowned by a giant wedding cake, gone aground. A line of pregnant Maya women poured out of the grandiose church, from an adjoining health clinic. When I asked about family planning, the nurse said they only provided delivery services. Across the plaza from the church, ranchers wearing straw hats and carrying machetes were gathered at a public meeting to get seedlings to replant the forests wiped out by recent landslides from the torrential rains brought on by Hurricane Stan. The idea of faith as survival was in play. Signs reading "Jesus is the Lord of San Pedro," and in "In God We Trust," were posted like Coca-Cola ads in shop windows.

Twenty minutes away, in Santiago, pinched between the San Pedro and Toliman volcanoes, there was an air of festivity. Beneath a miniature Ferris-wheel, a swarm of market ladies, with orange discs for headdresses, sold chicken feet and dried fish next to American pop CDs and knockoff shoes. Masked dancers performed as shamans on the colonial church steps. At the far end of the steps, next to three snarling curs, a blind man, eating cotton candy, shook his cup for money. A cadre of woodcutters, men with machetes and their backs loaded with fresh-cut tinder, passed by. A memorial to Father Stanley Rother, a priest from Oklahoma who was gunned down in the church by military assassins for his support of the local Tz'utujil-speaking Maya, was inscribed in stone near the front of the church, below which his heart is now buried.

A hotbed of Indian discontent, Santiago is now host to over thirty evangelical and Pentecostal churches, from at least twenty different sects. Many *atitecos*, as locals are known, converted to Protestant sects for protection, to avoid the ungovernable wrath of the army, whose tactics have repeatedly blurred the line between saintly and psycho.

If killing had become a way of life in Santiago, martyrs were the measure of its worth. In the "Peace Park," where the Guatemalan army encamped until 1990, is a memorial for thirteen locals, all Catholic, who were shot down during an unarmed protest that included hundreds of evangelicals and Catholics uniting in common cause. Every day since the massacre, food and rum and Cokes are placed on each of the thirteen stone markers.

"During the war we all thought it was an internal problem," Abraham (not his real name), a twenty-something activist, told me. "Since then we have learned more about American involvement in the murders." With a long family history here, Abraham wears a ponytail and gives off a Zen-like countenance. He is a field represen-

111

tative for World Neighbors, a nonsectarian charity. (The author served on the NGO's board of directors.)

Not far from where the "Atitlan Massacre" took place, down the pine forested-slopes of the Toliman Volcano, was a clean, earthen swath that could be mistaken for a perfectly cut logging road. In actuality, it was the unforgiving path of the 2005 mudslide that buried 700 people at three in the morning while they slept, turning the village of Panabaj, within the municipality of Santiago, into a graveyard. Over four thousand people in this larger Santiago community of 30,000 residents were left homeless. Maize and bean crops were destroyed. A year and a half later, the impact area still had the somber whiff of a cemetery, a recent Pompeii.

○ ○ ○

World Neighbors has been working in Guatemala since the early '70s. Its focus on "empowering locals" to solve their own problems of poverty, disease and hunger was never popular here with the government. Out of a modest, low-profile office near the center of Santiago, the NGO coordinated with a local partner to assist in the relief efforts. Sustainable development, identifying local leadership and inspiring self-reliance is World Neighbor's bread and butter, not disaster relief.

When I visited World Neighbor's offices in Guatemala, regional staff from Honduras were participating in a baseline study that addressed such problems as the "brown streak" around the lake (from soil erosion, hazardous insecticides and deforestation), crop and animal diseases, the shortage of low-interest credit lines for farmers, gender equality, food security, maximizing crop yields and agricultural diversity. Another World Neighbor's survey of farm ownership revealed that ninety percent of the workers are local, while their land ownership is only ten percent, a recipe for discontent.

The first step of solving poverty is putting money in the hands of poor people. Small community projects like fish farms, bee hives and high value fruit and vegetables not only increase food security but provide an income from selling the excess. Most small farms in the region grow maize and beans, which is consumed locally or sold at thin margins, whereas ninety-five percent of coffee is exported at tidy profits. The World Neighbor's study also showed high crop losses due to insects and storage damage, both of which are easily resolved. If Indigenous farmers were better organized, as they are (or once were) in the U.S., they could minimize the middle-man profits. Historical legacies and cultural complexities are the big hurdles that make success in local projects, sometimes but not often, as elusive as the Holy Spirit.

After an office lunch with World Neighbor's staff, Abraham and I walked two blocks to a different kind of temple and deity: Maximon, whose syncretic character embodies African Santeria, the Apostle Simon Peter, conquistador Pedro de Alvarado, and the pre-Columbian *costumbre* (traditional rites) that conjures the Maya Earth Lord, Ma'am. In the Lent season, the raffish, cigar-smoking, rum-drinking Maximon, also referred to as "Little Brother Simon," is trotted out in Santiago and other Maya settlements during processions of the Via Dolorosa as the biblical Judas, the anti-Christ, balancing the polarities of good and evil, of Spanish and Indian, of Catholics and Protestants. A trickster at heart, his effigy is often found on altars in Maya homes, businesses, bars and brothels, among all classes of people, from pickpockets and prostitutes and priests to farmers, traders and professionals. A *limpia*, or cleansing ceremony of Maximon, burning copal incense, making altar gifts, purifying the mind with kush, anointing oneself with *amour de l'otto* perfume, is said to have made barren women fertile, to have helped the diseased, handicapped and war weary, to have turned around teetering mom-and-pop businesses and pushed up modest agricultural yields into bumper crops.

A soiled red tapestry hung across the doorway leading into Maximon's temple, with balloons festooning the threshold. Inside, sitting half-slumped on a couch were Maximon's caretakers, sloshed on rum and kush. The air was sated with the robust scent of rum, copal incense, candle and cigar smoke, a chapel-like cross between a cantina and an opium den. The deity's handlers are members of one of ten Santiago *cofradios*, Maya Catholic religious brotherhoods that operate somewhat like Shriners, with both cabalistic secrecy and a spirit of largesse.

As I took a seat on a couch, one by one a line of adherents knelt at the altar, prayed to the folk saint, made contributions of quetzals, and knocked back thimbles of kush. A gem of a saintly image, Maximon's outlandishly rococo get-up included two Stetsons, a wildly patterned blue sash, a chest full of Salvation Army-grade ties, and a red, white and blue tunic with a gold cape flowing off his stack of Stetsons. A stubbed cigar, the ashes of which are saved as a cure for influenza, was crammed stooge-like into his mouth. Opposite Maximon was a recumbent Jesus in a glass sarcophagus, covered in plastic flowers and bookended by crucifixes of St. Andrew. Plastic grapes and creepers with flashing fairy lights hung like mistletoe from the ceiling, while "Rudolph the Red-Nosed Reindeer" and "We Wish You a Merry Christmas" played on a jam box. The baked in mood was equal portions party and piety. The whole razzle-dazzle harked of a Salvador Dali saying: "Take me, I am the drug."

Back in Antigua, it was the second Sunday of Lent, three more to go before Palm Sunday. The holy spirit was rising like a runaway fever. Cowboy and I walked to the village church of Jocotenango (meaning place of many jocotes), which melds seamlessly into Antigua. Along the way, locals poured out of homes and businesses, leveling the cobblestone streets with precision-drawn and vividly colored sand and sawdust carpets, known as *alfombras*, taking up to twenty-four hours to fashion. Slowly, meticulously, sprinkling, patting, painting, spraying, adorning the edges in offerings of fruits, vegetables, flowers, roses, carnations, bougainvillea petals, and *coroso*

(a white pungent fiber), Maya and ladinos worked against the clock to have their thirty-foot stretch of road ready at the unique moment the procession passes. Cowboy surveyed one carpet, piled with offerings of new potatoes, radishes, lettuce, carrots, and cauliflower, and wondered aloud what a Nicoise salad had to do with Easter.

Alfombra is derived from Arabic, so it was no wonder that each cobbled street took on the dazzling visage of a carpeted royal causeway out of a Scheherazade tale. But this was not the idle rich gathering for some palace intrigue, these were mostly Bruegel's sad-faced peasants paying penance in labor and quetzales, praying to wooden statues that they believe will lift them from their dire straits.

As we approached the central park, facing the bold pink Temple of Our Lady of the Assumption, clouds scattered and the sky turned a salutary powder blue. A sea of violet heaved at the doorway of the baroque church as the purple-robed *cucuruchos*, the carriers of the Passion float (*anda*), gathered, while inside Pontius Pilate and the Sanhedrin condemned the Messiah. Outside, and in all directions, a carnival-like atmosphere charged the air. An old Maya woman sat in the dust selling bananas and mangoes, another vendor peddled prayer beads and crucifixes, and countless others offered pizza, roasted chicken and fish on a stick. There was a merry-go-round for small children, and hockey and video games for the bigger ones.

When the trumpet sounded at eleven, thousands crushed together, praying in a mélange of Maya dialects and Spanish, the poorest living on the lowest base level of Abraham Maslow's hierarchy of needs giving the most to faith. God bless them, a confederacy of the humbled. I was in the middle, squeezed between two Maya women, short in stature, wearing woven blouses and wraparound skirts, their hair in braids. Worlds apart, yet pressed against my front side, was a twenty-something ladino woman in a halter top and blue jeans, holding a cell phone up high, clicking photos. The pageantry that followed was a transcendental scene that surely inspired billionaire

115

Roman Catholic Mel Gibson, anti-semitic Hollywood actor and director, to make "The Passion of the Christ," which grossed more than 600 million dollars.

Out of a blue fog of incense, Roman soldiers in leather leggings, skirts, shields, lances and helmets, with red cockades, flanked the forty-foot long, 7,000-pound wooden anda. The float was lofted shoulder high by the hooded, purple-robed cucuruchos, who are born into the brotherhood that cares for and carries the heavy platform each season. Solemn as death, the cucuruchos each wore crucifixes, inching forward, swaying on the uneven cobblestones, in a human tide of penance-paying participants and onlookers. Other cucuruchos, bearing long poles, lifted utility wires, opening the way for the twelve-hour journey to Antigua's symbolic Golgotha.

Three larger-than-life vignettes, an animated short version of the story in the Apostle's Creed, played out atop the anda: Pontius Pilate condemns a kneeling Jesus of Nazareth; the Messiah stands on a red Hebrew Bible, wearing a gold filigreed cape and crown of thorns, half-slumped from the weight of the cross; and an angelic figure stands over the fires of Hell, awaiting the Messiah to ascend from the dead. Stoking the Maya's atavistic memory, the Via Dolorosa and the ubiquitous and grotesquely bloodied statues of Jesus of Nazareth are said to give the Maya the jarring impression of ritual sacrifice.

A brass band of tubas, trumpets and trombones played and the bell tower rang while the Maya spectators stood stock-still, their dark humble faces twisted in severe expressions. There were more clouds of incense, and then out of the church came the Mater Dolorosa, the Virgin Mary, wearing a scarf and pink and green robes, shouldered by women all dressed in white. Faster and faster the drums were pounded, horns blew louder, while the belfry tower chimed in a crescendo of near rapture. Then, once the procession was away from the church, the uncountable moving mob took on a different energy, less doleful, more festive, falling in behind the andas along the embroidered roads, claiming the offerings of food. Some were on crutches and others were in wheelchairs, while the aged shuffled by. Garbage trucks followed, sweeping up the countless hours of toil and sacrifice in a matter of minutes.

Cowboy and I circled the village, stopping briefly at a wooden, one-room evangelical church (Ministerios El Calvarios Internacio). Surrounded by placards of the Passion, the fire-and-brimstone preacher had the packed house in a Pentecost-like state of ecstasy, dancing and swaying from side to side, raising their hands with palms up, singing an antiphonal chorus and shouting hallelujahs. We didn't understand the words so much, but we got the music and message. Outside the procession was passing by, with more horns and drums. The cacophony was almost drowned out by the driving din of the evangelicals, but no one quit singing or swaying; instead their intensity seemed to surge. Semana Santa (Easter Week), I was told, all this frenetic energy and fanfare rises to the tenth power, the Passion on acid. Cortes needed no statues or monuments to be remembered by. He is present in everyone's life here.

❂ ❂ ❂

Late that afternoon, at the police station next to the central plaza, two German women in their sixties or early seventies, stopped us and asked if we were going to the "Hill of the Cross," which overlooks Antigua. We weren't but officials suggested that because of bandits, or *ladrones*, tourists should not go without a police escort. "What do you mean Kemosabe," Cowboy blurted out, "there are Indians up there." *The Lone Ranger* humor failed to register.

On this festival day the police were shorthanded at the station, so Cowboy and I agreed to make the thirty-minute walk with the Germans. We learned that the women had been to Nicaragua on a donor mission for a charity that builds houses and promotes sustainable agriculture. As we walked, Sylvia, the blond, heavy-set one of the two told us she'd grown up in a convent, but after leaving at age seventeen, gave up religion. They had not been to the procession, nor heard about it, but when I showed her my digital images, Sylvia gasped, "Oh, the Passion, the Passion," almost wistfully, seeming to evoke some long-ago memory of her convent days.

They both wanted to know why Bush, who had arrived the day before, had come to Guatemala. "He has done nothing for these people," Sylvia protested. She then told us, with undisguised glee, that they had just heard that protesters were burning an American flag in front of the embassy in Guatemala City. It was a lot to digest in the same breath, the beauty of the Passion, the hostile politics, and thieves preying on the most vulnerable.

As we crested the hilltop overlooking Antigua and the cobalt blue lines of the Agua volcano, a senora screamed from behind me. In the next split second, two good-sized hombres bounded by us, fleeing into the woods. The woman had a baby, and the ladrones had stolen her bag with cell phone and camera in it. A local man came up, speaking snippets of English, to tell us that four more thieves were waiting for us in the forest along the path down. Suddenly Cowboy and I looked like knight-errants, chivalrous gringo heroes as we escorted the Germans, the ladino lady and her baby back with us. Other than the informant trying to shake us down, we had no more problems, but it did have the whiff of a police scam.

◎ ◎ ◎

At four in the morning we caught a small, twenty-passenger bus on to Honduras. I sat on the front row, facing a dark-skinned plastic Jesus on the dashboard. I felt the warmth, falling asleep in snatches with an earworm of Paul Newman strumming a banjo: I don't care if it rains or freezes/As long as I got my plastic Jesus... The music took me home, out of my loneliness in the wee hours. By noon we would be in the ancient Maya metropolis of Copan.

On board were two Kiwis and an Argentine couple, and we picked up six ladinos and a Honduran woman, Carla, in Guatemala

City. At first light we stopped for a food and fuel break. Cowboy and I sat at a counter next to Carla, a talkative grad student who was studying environmental science. We ordered corn tamales and tortillas and eggs, while she told us about the deforestation in Guatemala and Honduras. "Ninety percent of the forests in both countries have disappeared because the peasants use wood for cooking," she said. She talked about the need for renewable energy, as well as the slow-burning trash middens surfacing everywhere in Latin America. We were all ears.

Carla had purchased the morning's *Prensa Libre*, a daily Guatemalan newspaper. The first eight pages gave coverage of Bush's visit two days before. As it turned out, there wasn't just an American flag burned as Sylvia, the German woman, had told us. Demonstrators had also tossed eggs, firecrackers, stones and makeshift aerosol flamethrowers. On the front page was a photo of a throng of campesino protesters, including young girls and boys, holding up a banner, according to Carla's translation, that described Bush as "the snake that licks our boots." Cordoned by riot police, who broke out their cudgels on one group of angry protesters, other banners spoke of "genocide." One banner that wrapped around a crowd of hundreds was up to fifty feet long, stood head tall, and had Bush's face photo-shopped into that of Hitler. "Fascista" and "criminal" were written across it. The headline above the Nazi-inspired banner said, "Bush, go home."

The two Kiwis took the paper after us, and, laughing at the photos, said almost in unison, "That is why we only stopped in Los Angeles for one hour on our way to Mexico."

As Elizabeth Bell back in Antigua had predicted, before leaving Guatemala Bush had promised the military four helicopters and ship navigation systems to fight the "war on drugs." His commitment to help develop Latin America, from six years before, was not on the table. And relief for 300-plus illegal Guatemalan immigrants, who were at that moment being deported from the U.S., was shrugged off.

Some say Bush angered the gods here. At Iximche, in the Maya highlands, Indian priests, as superstitious as medieval peasants, held a special cleansing ceremony "to purify" the ancient temple the American president had visited. Near the temple, donning a traditional tunic, promoting the benefits of free trade, Bush had helped farmers load crates of lettuce for ten minutes at an Indigenous cooperative. Those photo ops, however, did nothing to alleviate the pervasive poverty.

❂ ❂ ❂

This was the third time I had been in a country when Bush arrived. Each time the reaction had been widespread, anti-America protests. In contrast, on two occasions—in Uganda and Vietnam—I was present when Clinton visited and the response was the opposite, an outpouring of goodwill. It comes down to development assistance known as soft power or diplomacy in which other nations are co-opted to sympathize with our values and customs versus weapons of war, hard power, ordering others to do what we want. A leg up for the poorest, a no-brainer if the brave and noble government servants working in hot spots around the world for USAID (United States Agency for International Development) are given the green light. (In 2025, the agency was gutted by President Donald Trump and billionaire Elon Musk.)

Politics in Latin America are instinctively anti-gringo, and when Bush or any other perceived adversary comes to town they stand up to America with increasing bravado. It didn't help that Fidel Castro wannabe President Hugo Chavez of Venezuela had been shadowing Bush's Latin American tour, speaking to adoring crowds in Argentina, Bolivia, Nicaragua, Jamaica and Haiti. U.S. expats and we travelers abroad miss the days when citizens of host countries waved the American flag to honor a visiting U.S. president, instead of burning it.

120

Chapter Five

"HE WALKS LIKE A COWBOY, maybe Clint Eastwood," said Marvin Diaz, a guide at the Maya ruins of Copan, commenting on Cowboy's distinctive swagger. Cowboy had heard it before. He chortled and kept walking, having already arranged with a local *gaucho* to go for a ride in the hills surrounding Copan. He was wearing his newest straw rancher's hat, bought in Antigua.

A half-dozen well-fed macaws perched on a fence in the shade near the entry gate. The macaw is Honduras's national bird; its vibrant plumage of red, yellow and blue were the color scheme for ancient Copan. As we listened to these New World parrots chatter, whistle, squawk and scream, Marvin, at six feet tall, an anomaly among his fellow Hondurans of Maya descent, described Copan as the Paris of the Maya Empire and King "18 Rabbit" as the Louis XIV of this pre-Columbian city-state. "It's the details here," he assured us, "that make it so unique." Marvin was talking about the portrait stelae and sculptured decorations found in the plazas and acropolis, some of which are still shaded in cinnabar red, a pentimento of former times. The habituated macaws seemed to scold us, raising the chatter level as we walked away toward the Great Plaza, partly shaded by a giant ceiba.

The Copan Valley was first settled in 900 B.C., but classical dynastic rule began around 426 A.D. upon the arrival of Great Sun Lord Quetzal Macaw, who held an alliance with Tikal and possibly Teotihuacan's indefatigable Fire is Born.

Hieroglyphics of dots and bars for counting, a right-turning swastika symbolic of the king, a stylized stela of 18 Rabbit, and a series of bas reliefs depicting sun and rain and monkey gods, fell across the plaza. Unlike Greeks and Romans, who used statuary for casual affectations, Maya artists cast their kings, cut free of the stone mass, in dignified frontal poses.

From atop the acropolis we overlooked the Copan River Valley. Maya kids swam and women bathed and washed clothes in the murky waters. Fields of jalapeno peppers, tobacco, and maize grew along the littoral, and shaved, earthen-covered mountaintops, sparsely seeded in plots of corn, receded into the haze. Along the side of the acropolis, marking 400 years of dynastic rule, was a bas relief of the sixteen great kings of Copan. In ancient times the city extended across the valley, but the course of the river shifted, burying or destroying much of Copan. The sweeping panorama we were taking in made up only twenty percent of its former grandeur.

We paused, getting a sense of the ambiance, absorbing the vibes around 18 Rabbit's tomb and the Jaguar Court (signified by a carved likeness). Stepped pyramids formed a quadrangle below where ritual ceremonies took place with the sounds of kettle drums, clay flutes, and gourd rattles, along with dancing, animal sacrifice and human bloodletting. Following Marvin Diaz's narrative of these festivities, tongue and penis pricking—returning the blood to the gods—was accompanied by the ingestion of psychotropic drugs, the Maya equivalent of psilocybin mushrooms and peyote.

Cowboy hypothesized, with some confidence, that 18 Rabbit was kicking up his buzz with a tankard of chocolate, mixed with honey. Marvin nodded his head in agreement, and pointed out that a loin-clothed 18 Rabbit was no paper tiger. As the high priest and lord, the Oz behind the curtain, he would have emerged for the ceremony out of a giant, carved serpent's head, from precisely where we were standing, wearing an ogre mask and jaguar skin headdress with iridescent quetzal plumes to lead the ritual—a breaking-the-fourth-wall mise en scène that we imagined would make an Alice Cooper or KISS concert seem mundane.

Opposite and below was the Central Plaza, which included a manicured pitch and the pelota court, said to be the largest of its time. Fronting a stela that depicted scenes of "materializing beings of the Otherworld" was a cosmic turtle altar, circled by a smooth runnel for blood to flow out onto the earth. Marvin briskly reminded us that bloodletting (or phlebotomy), though not used for the holistic belief of nurturing the gods, was also accepted medical practice in ancient Rome, Greece and Mesopotamia, and remained so in Europe until the 19th century.

Possibly the grandest achievement of Copan is the Hieroglyphic Stairway, a flat-topped pyramid of sixty-three steps and 2,200 glyphs. A Maya bible, encyclopedia and work of art all in one, rising from the plaza, now sheltered beneath a fiberglass protective roof. The step-pyramid was built by King Smoke Shell, who was commemorated in opposing stelae, one facing the rising sun and the other the setting sun. The king is youthful in one stele, holding the royal scepter, a double-headed serpent bar, and aged in the other, an old man with a Fu Manchu moustache and wispy beard, shaded with the original cinnabar red paint, appearing remarkably Chinese.

While Cowboy bolted off to meet a man about a horse (not a drug deal), I circled Copan Ruinas, the 1890s village that sprang up a half-mile from the ancient city-state to accommodate archaeologists and tourists. With cattle ranches and maize farms disappearing through the mountain valleys in all directions, the village was full of gauchos in straw hats. There was even a pasture of several well-gaited bays on the edge of town. The gauchos, lurking around the tiendas and bank, all arrived by horse. One street had a row of bohemian artists selling handmade jewelry and paintings. Nearby was an alleyway with a covered market offering carvings and textiles, but no tourists.

A block away in the central plaza two mimes entertained Maya kids. The performers were American, from Sebring, Florida, working for Editorial Bautista Independiente (EBI), publisher and distributor of conservative Bible-based material in Spanish. As fast as their performance was over they each handed out cards and brochures.

The heat was stifling, slowing the pace at night in Copan Ruinas to a crawl, a lingering of a few diehard traders and scant outsiders. After his ride in the mountains, Cowboy met me in the Red Frog bar, where we drank Port Royal Pilsners with two locals. For an hour and a half, the rantings of a Honduran evangelist, preaching defiantly from a rostrum in San Pedro Sula, blasted on the television in the open-air, upstairs bar.

❂ ❂ ❂

The next morning Cowboy and I shouldered our bags and ambled down the dirt road to the new bus station, a covered row of benches and a ticket window next to a horse pasture. We were there for the daily bus to Tegucigalpa. Before boarding we were asked to step through a metal detector, after which a security woman with a digital camera took our photos. This was followed by a young man wearing a rent-a-cop uniform body searching us with all the bureaucratic surliness of an international airport. I could only guess that here in the Western Hemisphere's most malnourished country—its dictators distinguished as America's greatest ally in the region—that the bus station search was funded by the simultaneous U.S. wars on terror and drugs. It might also be part of the overall aid package given by the U.S. for the ongoing militarization of Honduras. Mercifully, we were cleared of any lawbreaking activities to board the bus on to Tegucigalpa. It was our first such search, not even a cursory look, in over 2,000 miles of bus riding.

Cowboy spread out in the first-class section, while I took a preferred seat a couple of rows behind him. The bus didn't fill up until we arrived in Santa Rosa an hour later. George, a pinch-faced former

Peace Corps volunteer in the Dominican Republic was sitting across the aisle. Since finishing his two years of service, mostly building fish farms on a USAID project, he told me he had been traveling with a couple of Argentine girls whom he'd met in Guatemala. He appended that the Argentines had not only been pleasantly surprised to meet a gringo who spoke Spanish, but they were rethinking their stereotype of all-Americans-are-brutes. I told him that seemed like a welcome break from the monolithic way of judging Americans or anyone else, then mused that typecasting those girls as members of Argentina's Death Squads would have never occurred to me.

Wending our way up pine-forested mountains or plunging down into valleys fed by fast moving streams, we passed countless campesino villages of *ranchos*, houses made of bamboo poles and roofs of leaves and sugarcane, woven together tightly to keep the rain out, with the occasional galvanized tin roof. Once in the heart of the Comayagua Mountains convoys of soldiers passed as frequently as herds of cattle, giving way only after being prodded and scattered by a gaucho bearing a long pole.

We were out of Maya territory; from here on the people were mostly *mestizos*, who make up ninety percent of Honduras's population. But that didn't change the frequency of corn plots or fields of bananas, which are as common in these parts as rice paddies are in Vietnam. After all Honduras was the original "Banana Republic," and underwent seven revolutions in a fifteen-year period that ended in 1907, underscoring its total dependence on foreign governments and an economy based on exporting one crop.

◊ ◊ ◊

The "Octopus," as Hondurans once called United Fruit Company, was a parallel government until 1954, when in a spontaneous show of defiance, 40,000 workers walked off their jobs on the fertile, Atlantic coast plantations. Four months later, United Fruit acceded to their demands—a modest wage increase, better

125

housing and medical care—arguably marking the beginning of a rising tide of unionism and revolution in Latin America and a precipitous slide in power and influence for United Fruit. These events, of course, also meant that campesinos lost their jobs because the whole system was corrupted.

A Taft-era U.S. consul in Tegucigalpa once quipped, "Buying a mule costs more than a Congressman." All that changed in 1975 when Eli Black, the President of United Brands (nee United Fruit), jumped to his death from his office window in New York's Pan Am Building. The heat was on over the $1.25 million bribe he had paid the Honduran president.

U.S. paternalism in Honduras and across Central America, led by military interventions and special interests like United Fruit, began in spirit with the chief advocate of America's policy of manifest destiny, Thomas Jefferson, who succinctly declared, "We have a hemisphere to ourselves." In 1813, as Simon Bolivar and his wars of liberation gave Latin America new hope, Jefferson was not so optimistic: "History...furnishes no example of a priest-ridden people maintaining a free civil government." The Monroe Doctrine came next, and when Soviet leader Nikita Khrushchev declared those principles of hemispheric dominance extinct almost a century and a half later, the U.S. State Department said they were as valid then as they were in 1823 when the doctrine was established.

With the building of the Panama Canal, President Theodore Roosevelt saw intervening in Central American revolutions as obligatory statecraft to keep the sea lanes secure and to protect the region's American investors who had seemingly become our national interest. Known as the Roosevelt Corollary, the U.S. became the region's policeman, but rarely in the service of the commonweal and democracy.

Over the course of the 20th century up to two-thirds of U.S. trade, including oil, passed through the Panama Canal. That alone provided the justification for blocking foreign concessions along the isthmus, for abrogating Pan-American treaties, and for disregarding regional court systems, while willy-nilly going at it with hammer and tong when the internal politics of a given country didn't go our way. Since 1898 not one of the forty governments the United States has overthrown in Latin America, mostly in the Caribbean-Central American region, became democratic, fulfilling Thucydides' millennia-old maxim of realpolitiks: The strong do what they can, and the weak suffer what they must.

Fair trade served up in Latin America meant that U.S. consumers got bananas and coffee at low prices, while American manufacturers exported their goods south at inflationary prices. Having it both ways was indeed the state of trade affairs through the '50s and '60s, setting the stage for the populist revolutions of the '70s and '80s. Controlling that imbalance with military interventions as both carrot and stick, promoting one-or-two-crop Latin American economies, was U.S. Foreign Policy 101.

There was ample precedent for such tactics in Washington. In 1911 President William Howard Taft sent marines into Honduras for two years to protect American banana interests. At the same time, more marines were dispatched to Nicaragua, where they stayed without popular local support for over two decades. With ninety-eight percent of the land owned by two percent of the people (and foreign investors), not just in Honduras but throughout Central America, foreign investors and consumers, local elites and the military have always been the beneficiaries.

By the 1930s the U.S. had developed a strategy of training local militaries to maintain stability. Franklin Roosevelt's well-intentioned Good Neighbor Policy became more about controlling military dictators who supported our special interests than about grass roots economic development. All of this militarization was done while under vehement protest by member nations of the Organization of American States (OAS). According to Walter Lafeber in his revealing book

Inevitable Revolutions, the School of Americas was not opened in the Panama Canal Zone for hemispheric protection, but for "internal security." The officer training center soon became known as the School of Golpes (Coups). When a Mexican official got wind of the American school, he quipped, "Give me the names of the first sixty students, and I'll pick your presidents in Latin America for the next ten years."

Militarizing Honduras meant taking a classless culture, where virtually everyone was poor but easygoing, and polarizing it by giving power to an American-made military oligarchy. Timelessly, as well as time and again, in Honduras and beyond, as the pressure of nationalism and income-inequality builds, revolutions have happened in the same gravitational way that engine gaskets blow: too much tension between countervailing forces.

During the '80s, with anti-American-inspired civil wars raging in Nicaragua, Guatemala and El Salvador, the U.S. oversaw the parallel repression of civil society in a neutral Honduras. We armed the dictator du jour and local National Guard to the teeth, constructed eleven airfields and two radar stations across the country, laid asphalt not through peasant regions but to the encircling war zones, and built Palmerolo Air Base, where Oliver North and Joint Task Force Bravo operated. Over 80,000 U.S. soldiers were sent on maneuvers there and untold Hondurans were trained. Honduras had become an American military redoubt. Now, with the costly and open-ended wars on drugs and terror, Palmerolo remains home to 1,200 to 1,500 American troops and Joint Task Force Bravo, as well as to the Honduran Air Force Academy, with a C-5 Galaxy-capable runway, a rarity in the region.

Although economic aid slowed opposition to the militarization of Honduras, in 1981, 60,000 demonstrators took to the streets in Tegucigalpa and 20,000 in San Pedro Sula, protesting the presence of 12,000 U.S.-supported contras who were encamped and operating out of Honduras. "Yankee Go Home!" was the clear message. In response,

128

the military captured and killed hundreds of protesters. For a country known for its tropical, laidback lifestyle, this was the first time in Honduran history for such widespread repression, a time when the average monthly income of campesinos was less than $25.

Elvia Alvarado, author of *Don't Be Afraid, Gringo*, which I was reading on the bus, was, like most Honduran campesinos, transformed by the arrogant actions of the U.S. in the '80s:

> If someone doesn't like what you are doing they label you a communist. But we campesinos aren't afraid of the Soviet Union. I've never seen a Soviet person in my life. But I've seen lots of gringos, almost all of them soldiers. So that's who we are afraid of—the United States.

> We campesinos don't care about communism or socialism. We don't understand what they mean. What we do understand is injustice. What we do understand is that we have to fight for the right to live like human beings. We don't care what you call it—capitalism, socialism, communism, any ism.

> ...Do you think a mother who can't send her children to school because she doesn't have any clothes to put on their back feels at peace? Do you think a mother who watches her child die because she doesn't have a penny to take her to the doctor feels at peace? ...To protect this great peace we have, the politicians have sold our country off to the United States.

❂ ❂ ❂

As we came into Tegucigalpa, a hundred or more protesters, employees of the Honduran electric utility company, marched down the middle of a busy four-lane road, waving signs and chanting. On one street corner young boys held up live iguanas for sale; on another a scruffy swarm of moneychangers waved their wads of lempira. Other than usual racket of touts and taxi drivers, it was all

129

peaceful as we arrived mid-afternoon at the downtown bus station. George, the Peace Corps volunteer, was staying where we were at the New Boston, so we shared a taxi.

The 1940s-era hotel was in a transitional neighborhood, dusty, noisy, a cat's cradle of electrical wiring, and full of loafers, toughs, and pickpockets. We had to ring a buzzer to get one of the two old ladies who ran the place to let us in. The rooms were spacious with high ceilings, but sterile with fussy care and an economy of furnishings. The always-watchful old ladies with faces like poached eggs gave us the feeling of entering a psychiatric ward. But we were there for only one night, then off to the south, near the El Salvador border, to a World Neighbors project.

Cowboy, jumpy as ever, buzzed off looking for a new wide-brimmed straw hat (he had bought six by now), while I went next door to a video arcade which had a few computers. The young man behind the counter showed me to a dust-laden Dell computer that looked more like an antique television. He told me he lived in Utah, that he was here vacationing for two weeks. His brother owned the arcade. The country is full of these relationships, due to the diaspora that started in the '70s and continues till this day. Remittances from the one million Hondurans now living in the U.S. total 2.5 billion dollars, or one-fourth of the country's GDP. Those were the lucky ones who made it out, while many remain stuck in the slums of Tegucigalpa, looking for work and a better life.

✪ ✪ ✪

Edwin Escoto, a thirty-five-year-old stocky mestizo and a program coordinator for World Neighbors, arrived the next morning at the New Boston in an aging Toyota pickup. Since his English was about as good as my Spanish, he called his wife to help us find a translator to ride along. Thirty minutes later, at a turnoff to the south, we drew to a stop where Karla Lopez waited with an overnight bag.

Karla, a cheery-faced twenty-year-old student in eco-tourism at the National University of Honduras, was eager to use her English. In the first few minutes of meeting, she told us that her father was a career, government-employed environmental engineer. She then beamed with pride, telling us in an unctuous manner about her American connection, an aunt, who has been married three times, and her cousins, all living in Houston. Karla had a better standard of living than most in Honduras. For now, her plans were to stay put and not join the brain drain that drives the educated in the Global South to migrate.

Navigating the gated neighborhoods and traffic jams of central Tegucigalpa, we drove through several miles of shanty villages, *barrios marginals* Karla called them. These barrios are where many who come to the city for opportunity wind up, toning down the dichotomy of rural and urban, and amping up vulnerabilities to crime and diseases like HIV/AIDs. For the first time in history, over fifty percent of the world's population now lives in urban areas. Although typically there is more money to be made in urban areas, when disaggregated from urban-versus-rural economic data, slums are poorer, hard-to-escape poverty traps.

The tin shacks covered in rocks to secure the roofs were upscale when compared to the lean-tos of cardboard and plastic and anything else they could pile on their minimalist shelters. Turkey buzzards circled over the smoldering trash heaps, competing with the rats and residents for edible refuse.

Further along, the sun was incandescent, scorching the barren mountains a dull brown, with a green ridgeline, a tuft of trees or garden plot here and there in the valleys. Streams were dry and rivers a languid gray but lined in a colorful patchwork of freshly-washed clothes. Most cattle and people along the river were motionless, inert like giant geckos. Chicken buses moved everywhere, groaning and spewing, while a few woodcutters on horseback came off the ridges laden with piles of kindling. Two hours later we arrived in Nacaome, a slumberous market town, where World Neighbors has a modest office in a home.

Emilio Agular, a twenty-nine-year-old agricultural specialist, who learned his job by attending World Neighbors technical trainings, arrived as we did on his company ride, a 100cc Suzuki motorbike. Emilio is from a small community in the precinct of Morocopay, where the World Neighbors project is focused. Ada Oseguera, who is in charge of healthcare training for the Morocopay villagers, awaited us in the office. Ada and Emilio owe their jobs to being leaders in World Neighbors target communities. Until now, as I began to drill down to the heart of the matter, my diary had the whiff of a landscape painter.

To understand World Neighbor's methodology, it helps to know the spirit in which it was founded. Dr. John Peters, an army chaplain in the Philippines in World War II, cradled in his arms a young soldier who had just been shot, and watched him die. "It would be like so many others," he said, recounting the letters to loved ones he had written as chaplain. "'He was a good soldier…died quickly, not knowing what hit him…bravely, in the line of duty…you can be proud…God sustain you.' What else could I say? But I was sick of saying it." Surrounded by abject poverty and witnessing the "wasteful" deaths of so many, he made himself a promise after the soldier died: "If I get out of this alive, I'm going to do something, somehow, somewhere, to help other people."

Dr. Peters was as good as his word. World Neighbors is now seventy-five years old and has served over twenty-five million impoverished people in more than fifty countries. Although Dr. Peters and all those who joined him had a steep learning curve, he knew from the "rice Christians" he had seen in Korea and the Philippines that you can't donate your way out of poverty, that all people cry out for dignity, that help is "tendered as a catalyst, not a cushion, a hand up not a hand out."

World Neighbors went through a collaborative process to iden-
tify a mobilizing theme in Morocopay, an area of acute poverty in a
country where over fifty percent of the population lives below the
poverty line. As a starting point, World Neighbors has a bias toward
agriculture, food security and community health interventions.
Leading with family planning in campesino villages, where evangelical preachers and Catholics priests are the thought leaders, will not
get a foot in the door.

In World Neighbors' experience community leaders like Emilio
and Ada, if open to fresh ideas about low-tech agriculture or sanitation
or hygiene, must then convince the rest of the village to go along
with what they suggest. At least half of the village is extremely wary
of all things foreign, especially if new. Focusing on building relationships on a village level, World Neighbors checkerboards target areas
such as Morocopay, working toward an irreversible critical mass that
transforms and catalyzes social change. After six to eight years, when
their work is done, they move on. Villages solving their own problems
of hunger, poverty and disease, neighbors helping neighbors.

❂ ❂ ❂

On the outskirts of Nacaome, Edwin goosed the Toyota, trailing
clouds of dust, into the ecologically fragile mountainous terrain. The
most fertile land along the Choluteca River and nearby coastal plains
amounts to a mere twenty percent of Honduras's total landmass and
is the domain of coffee and fruit companies and the wealthy *latifun-
distas* (estate owners). Skirting that fertile crescent, we passed through
a mean environment, dry as a bone and hard-baked by the sun, along
a washboard road that hadn't seen a grader in months or years. A few
miles from the World Neighbors project area, Emilio pointed out
the stubs of a former orchard. "Last week the farmer cut down nine
fruit trees so he could have wood for cooking," he told us.

Denuded hillsides plunged into narrow, uninhabited seams and
chasms like axe clefts in the earth. There was no reforestation, just

cutting, like milking a cow but never feeding it. "Where was the advantage?" Cowboy kept repeating, bumfuzzled by why World Neighbors would choose to work in such a dust bowl (or that anyone would want to live here). The homes, or ranchos, were made of mud and bamboo and thatch, a forage-starved goat here, a scrawny cow over there. Common sense told us, looking in from the outside, that humans aren't like bacteria and they can't just mutate and adapt to a wasted environment.

As we rocked along, Emilio told me about his brother, Luis, who has a wife and three kids living in Morocopay. For several years Luis had been working construction in Tegucigalpa, but inflation left him with nothing, the lempira having gone up 900 percent since the wars ended in 1990. Six months before an uncle loaned him $4,000 for the long trek *el norte*, through Guatemala and Mexico. Fortunately, Luis made it, and is now living in New York and working construction, paying off his uncle and hoping to put away enough to repatriate in a few years and get back to his wife and kids. With almost fifteen percent of Hondurans in the States, these stories abound of the American Dream.

A young village woman, wearing tight blue jeans and clutching two baby boys, stood beneath a *palapa*, an open-sided thatched roof bus stop, thumbing a ride. As Edwin geared down to a roll, Emilio jumped out and grabbed the youngest kid, while the adolescent woman climbed in the back with the other. According to Emilio, she was seventeen and had had her first baby at fourteen. "She's already divorced and remarried with a new child."

Karla wasn't surprised. "When they turn twelve here they are thinking about marriage and babies," she told us. And campesino men are notorious for leaving their wives, having a honeymoon in the corn patch, and starting a new family. Of course, once these young girls are pregnant, they don't have an ice cube's chance in hell of having a better life, and school is out forever.

134

We rose higher, and crest by crest the bald-topped mountains fell in misty waves to the sea until the hinterlands of El Salvador and the imposing hulk of Tiger Island came into view. During the civil war, lasting from the late '70s till the early '90s, the U.S. installed sophisticated eavesdropping equipment on the volcanic island; it doubled as a refuge for the Contras.

We stopped in El Rincon, a village of thirty-six homes, mostly stucco with painted floors and corrugated clay-tiled roofs. The village was surrounded by fruit and vegetable gardens so lush they created a canopy effect—the shade cooling the air and slowing evaporation. It was an oasis topped by a twenty-foot water tower built with a grant from the Nacaome municipality. There was no electricity here. Electric power, along with clinics, schools, and water systems will only happen, if ever, after years and years of fighting *caciques* (political bosses) and a corrupt bureaucracy.

A pile of fresh-cut striplings lay near the front door of a home near the baize-painted water tower. A shirtless and shoeless Julio, forty-one, and Nicola, thirty-six, barefoot and cradling a puling baby, greeted us beneath a mango tree, as the younger ones of their brood of six circled warily, studying the aliens with embryonic eyes. Given the high infant mortality rate, Ada said she would be surprised if Nicola hadn't lost at least one child.

As many children as there were in Morocopay, for the two days I visited I didn't see a single kid with the telltale signs of unhealthy diets or poor hygiene—swollen bellies, ginger hair, rheumy eyes. They were dirt poor, but between the nutrition, hygiene and other healthcare trainings set up by Edwin and the weekly visits by Emilio and Ada, living conditions had radically improved in six short years.

Before going inside, we walked by a compost pile, by banana and papaya trees and the spare branches of a small fruit that tasted like sour apples, and by plots of sugarcane, corn, beans, and peppers, all grown organically. Everything is low-tech here, no fertilizer, and no tractors or motorized tillers. There may be an occasional ox, but more often farmers use bare hands and primitive tools for digging. Emilio provides these small subsistence farmers with the best seeds, but after the first harvest, he asks them to pass their gift on to a neighbor. This is the same tried-and-true strategy employed by the Heifer Foundation, which works in partnership with World Neighbors. Heifer donates a cow or goat or water buffalo, and when the animals have offspring, the family gives it to a neighbor—the gift that keeps on giving.

A parakeet swooshed and shrieked by and yellow-breasted blackbirds pecked the scrub beyond the garden. The grounds around the house were so clean they looked like a just-swept porch. A bamboo-latticed latrine was set away from the house, near the garden, as was a chicken coop and pen with a crude roof for a single milk cow...not the customary barnyard frolic of Third World villages. About this time, Cowboy seized on the obvious, that Julio and Nicola had only two acres. Subdividing it six ways every generation would be problematic (if not Malthusian).

At the doorway, crude stepping stones had been removed and recently replaced by a raised patch of nicely graded terra firma so the youngest kids wouldn't fall and cut themselves, and to stave off standing water around the house that might attract insects. Inside, separated by curtains, mattresses rested on an earth-tone-painted floor that felt like hard clay. Mosquitoes and bedbugs, or *chinches*, are a huge problem. "Big blood-suckers," Julio said, with a grimace. Painting, organizing, boiling water, and recycling food waste and water were the small improvements that had only recently become accepted practice. An earthen stove stood in the corner of the user-friendly kitchen, with a newly-cut window next to it. The ventilation will reduce respiratory problems that are otherwise common among campesinos. A few pots and pans hung from the earthen wall, with a battery-powered radio beneath.

In Morocopay, they depend on a radio for news, education, and public service announcements such as storm warnings. Given the high rates of illiteracy, newspapers are not an option, and the Morocopay school only goes to the sixth grade. After that the only education available is on Saturday morning via radio. Other than a change of clothes hanging on a couple of hooks, that was the sum of Julio and Nicola's abode.

Two years before, Julio had worked construction in Tegucigalpa to get the money to build his simple house. Now, he returns to the city for two months each year, bringing home $250, which is the family's annual budget. That money, an exceptionally nice night out for my wife and me in Boston, must buy a year's worth of cooking oil, rice, soap, coffee, books and clothes for school. When food costs—sixty to eighty percent of a campesino's budget—increase in this less-than-a-dollar-a-day world, shortages occur and bring on social unrest. In any given year, Julio says books and school fees get cut first.

Nicola has had all six babies on these grounds, all delivered by midwives. Ada says most of the midwives are too old to keep up the rigorous demands of the profession. Looking ahead, Ada has held several midwifery trainings for younger women, whom she hopes will take over soon. Ada's workshops on family planning and reproductive health are an uphill battle. At the evangelical church down the road, the preacher counsels the villagers to "accept the children that God sends you."

After this last baby, Nicola had a tubal ligation, and now sees a doctor for an annual examination. Delicate as it was to discuss, particularly with Julio, both events were breakthroughs, especially in a machismo culture where husbands are jealous of doctors, where family planning is rumored to cause cancer, where more kids join the work force and provide social security in old age, where paying health costs and doctors' fees is a luxury. And then, of course, there is the church. Even Karla, educated, citified, and from a small family, echoed the biblical message of the evangelical preacher: "As a Catholic I believe you take what God gives."

Ada, who has two kids and a third on the way, aptly describes the local objections to family planning as religious and cultural (a hard egg to unscramble). She has brought in local preachers and priests for classes in community health, but they remain stuck in a narrow and selective interpretation of Biblical writings. Like many ancient traditions here, such as contour farming or sophisticated canal and irrigation systems, the use of birth control was lost back in pre-Columbian times, when it was used to keep the population in balance with the land. Still, every few months Ada holds family planning workshops targeting twelve- to eighteen-year-old girls. With the combination of sexual health education and the availability of contraception, she believes the rate of unplanned pregnancies is falling.

We drove a short way to Francisca's home, which had been vastly improved. She was spreading her wash across a crude fence of striplings as we talked. Her three youngest kids played out back. At age thirty-eight, Francisca has at least six children, and was pregnant again. When I asked where the older ones were, she said that two boys had gone to Tegucigalpa for work. A few minutes later, her husband Nicolas arrived, joining us for the ride down to the newly constructed tilapia pond. Twelve families, or over 100 people, had come together six months ago with the help of a thousand-dollar loan from a community credit savings plan (like micro-financing but using the participants' money), and paid a dozer operator from Nacaome to dig the spring-fed pond.

Tilapia, from fingerlings to twelve-inchers, churned the pond's jade-colored waters, hitting the surface to feed on corn. The campesinos' returns on investment were growing by the day. Circling the pond were a dozen or so men, all darkened by the sun, lean, red-blooded masculinity, hardworking and most likely equally as hard-drinking. They seemed to exude pride but it could just as easily have

138

been paranoia, as they appeared to be spaced in uneven yet discrete intervals, perhaps staking out their claim to a slice of the pie.

Alberto, with Marlboro-Man-sculpted good looks, wearing a white straw hat, and smelling of moonshine, told me he had ten kids, but never would say from how many women. He did, however, sound like the consummate family man when he told me, "I am responsible for my family and the pond makes us more secure. We know the fish will be fresh, not like at the market, and my kids won't get sick. And, we can sell what we don't eat."

Another Morocopay community has already picked up on the tilapia farm idea and built one too, starting the multiplier effect, providing a reliable source of protein to supplement their staple diet of beans and corn tortillas.

At least ten people jumped on the dusty rucksacks in the back of the truck, catching a lift to various villages along the road to Nacaome. Alberto rode with us in the cab, and as we drove into the sunset, facing El Salvador's frontier, he told me about the bomb explosions they once heard not far from where we were. Edwin said there were many landmines left behind along the border. For now, Tiger Island was washed in golden splendor, brilliant as the plumes of a quetzal as the sunset spread like wings across the water. In the flush of twilight beauty, I understood why the villagers of Morocopay called this home and didn't want to leave. As the poet Bob Dylan sings, "beauty walks a razor's edge."

◈ ◈ ◈

By seven the next morning Raul was outside the only guest house in Nacaome waiting for us. Edwin had driven back to Tegucigalpa the night before after dropping us off. Later in the day we were catching a chicken bus with Karla, but only after we visited a few more villages in Morocopay.

Raul, who has ten kids, six of whom migrated to Tegucigalpa for work and one who made it to San Francisco, thought of the world as his oyster. After all he was gainfully employed as a driver, had a son in the States sending money home, and his house was the first to have electricity in Morocopay. He helped to install it, and for that, got free service for one year (for a single light bulb).

Like the day before, within minutes my clothes, hair, mouth, nose, ears, and all pores were covered and clogged with powdery red dust. Washboarding along, we passed two hillside farms, one spotted in white wooden boxes of beehives, the other with the apiary in a custom-built shed. Raul told us that after attending the first bee-farming workshop everyone was afraid to handle the bees. Allaying their fears, Emilio talked to the communities about the economic benefits and two villages took the leap. By no great surprise, the ancient Maya were beekeepers and kept records of honey and beeswax production, but the practice was lost when their culture was destroyed.

Raul brought us to a stop at a sharp turn in the road below a steep incline that was so lush in banana trees that there was shade all around. Nearby, a new fifty-foot community water well had recently been dug. On that day it served as the village news center. Cackling and soaping, two women washed off in an open brick perimeter while two others stood by balancing water buckets on their heads, pitching in their two cents. Deora, a forty-two-year-old mother of seven, aged well beyond her biological years, arrived, introduced herself and directed us up a path to her home and expansive garden. Her husband was in Nacaome for the day.

Deora beamed with pride as she walked us through a forest canopy of banana, yucca and papaya trees, long trellises of grapes, and plots of corn, peppers, beans and tomatoes. In her worldview we were strolling through Tara, and from what Cowboy and I had seen of the area, she was justified. Aside from her family's hard work and attending a few workshops, a 7,000-liter catchment tank fed by an underground spring was making all this possible. Over fifty percent

140

of the family's harvest was now sold in the market. Not only has her family become more self-reliant, it is verging on middle-class for Honduras. They have more money for meat, for education and medicine, for land and cows and goats, for milk and honey.

But Cowboy, who can lull you into thinking he's just a slow-talking, cracker-barrel raconteur, not paying attention, obsessively honed in on the upside and downside of these tiny family farms (on which he came of age). "How do you keep dividing these small plots of land?" he repeatedly asked, not seeing it through the eyes of a harmonic balance, of giving people hope, but through the raw matrix of numbers that drive business decisions. He was right. Bearing in mind the health and food security successes, when set against the unexpected hurricane or war, and without effective family planning, it's like digging a hole and filling it up.

Deora's nineteen-year-old daughter, who had never been married but has two children, walked with us through the garden and house. Piled against the house were three freshly delivered plastic bags of rice and corn flour from Save the Children, a worldwide charity (NGO) that believes every child deserves a future. The rest of Deora's children were scattered; two had moved to Tegucigalpa for work. Deora had her tubes tied after her seventh child, but her daughter is doing nothing for birth control. Like almost everyone I talked to, Deora and her daughter gave me their preacher's tag line that children are a gift from God.

❁ ❁ ❁

The more I saw and heard, the more apparent it became that the families of Morocopay were trapped in a cycle of poverty and don't know it. It's a universal truth that with better women's education and a higher standard of living, families have fewer children, while lowering infant and maternal mortality rates. It's a universal myth that you can donate out of poverty, or that GDP growth, farming advancements, or free trade are the be-all and end-all. Aside from

141

the successes Deora's family has enjoyed, the people of Morocopay are fulfilling Malthus's theory—and Cowboy's business intuition.

An honest conversation with the church and with local, state and world leaders, about family planning (not abortion) and dispelling taboos about the structural socio-economic problems here are the 800-pound gorillas in Honduras and on the world stage. Ada, Emilio, Edwin and World Neighbors are doing their part, but where are the honest brokers that have it within their power to bring sustainable development to scale? Does anyone doubt for a moment that the flow to the urban slums of Tegucigalpa from Morocopay is as predictable as gravity? And that from there the lucky-ducks get to migrate on to the U.S.?

There's rarely any mention in the public square or media about the root causes of poverty in Latin America, or the retrograde positions evangelical and Catholic churches take on family planning. Much less any hard analysis or real political will to solve the problem of campesinos leaving their homeland for the U.S (the *Reconquista* as Mexicans call their migration north). Much too often the deluded thinking of the "haves" is that the "have-nots" are up to no good, gaming the healthcare, tax, welfare, and education systems. When I lived in Vietnam, which instituted successful family planning programs nationwide to stem post-war population growth, a local maxim held that to kill a snake you must step on its head and not its tail.

Long ago, Dr. Peters learned these truths, about all people needing dignity, about self-empowerment, about being in balance with the environment and not separate from it. Not because it was in the Scriptures, though he was a deeply religious, ethical and patriotic man, but because he was screaming from the rooftops with firsthand knowledge of the sufferings and reality of the world's poor people, and lifting a helping hand in empathy was the right thing to do. He lived his truth.

142

Nicaragua: From William Walker to Daniel Ortega

Chapter Six

THE CHICKEN BUS back to Tegucigalpa was crowded, at times both scary and liberating, careering around curves, the windows open wide. When we stopped for more passengers, a clown with a bulbous red nose, blue lips and potato-sack trousers boarded for the ride to the next village. He told jokes, performed silly tricks for the children, sold pencils and collected paltry tips from parents. Karla told us his jokes were bad, but Cowboy and I and the kids on board were amused.

After another night at the hospital-like New Boston, by nine the next morning we filed off the Tica bus we had boarded at sunrise and were standing in line at Nicaragua's border post. Trucks and buses queued up on the frontier crossing along with an army of money-changers, all armed with calculators and toilet-paper-roll-sized wads of tattered bills. Next were the DVD hawkers, the ice cream vendors, the beggar boys and the woman who wouldn't give up. Smashed on glue or moonshine, she was eight months pregnant. "You foreigner, *mucho dinero*, give me one dollar. I need for me and my baby," she said, over and over, pointing to her hump. Her jeans were unzipped, splayed open as if she had just come from a tryst in the bushes with one of the truckers. "Quit begging and go to work, wash clothes or something," the burly immigration officer told her, waving his hand to shoo her away like a stray dog.

✪ ✪ ✪

Welcome to post-civil war Nicaragua, I thought. It was back to the future: only a month before, former president and Cold War Sandinista leader Daniel Ortega had been re-inaugurated, for the first time in seventeen years. It wasn't a resounding victory, garnering only thirty-eight percent of the vote, but nonetheless while America focuses on wars in Iraq and Afghanistan, anti-Yankee Latin leftists win one election after another.

Venezuelan President Chavez, long-time promoter of Castro-style revolution in Latin America, had just left Managua a few days before our arrival on his anti-Yankee blitz. It was his way of taking the air out of Bush's Latin America "goodwill tour." Upon leaving the country, Chavez pledged millions more in aid money to Ortega and Nicaragua. That irresponsible largesse was in addition to the ten billion barrels of generously-financed oil he delivered each year to keep the local economy afloat. Any old half-wit could see it was only a matter of time until the Castro wannabe and his protege Nicolas Maduro would bankrupt Venezuela and send eight million refugees fleeing in all directions.

Power blackouts are common in Nicaragua, a deterrent to attracting foreign capital. At the same time, eighty percent of the six million Nicaraguans, or Nics as they're called, live on less than two dollars a day. That Ortega has been re-elected, while fifty percent of the country's wealth is in the hands of ten percent of the people, is a reminder of the century-old cycle of repression and revolution in Nicaragua.

✪ ✪ ✪

A few hours after catching the Tica bus at the border, we were taxiing through Managua traffic. Legless men in wheelchairs with their hands out and vendors selling fruit wine, parakeets, cashews and furry creatures the size of squirrels greeted us at stop lights. We passed a park full of baseball fields, compliments of American marines who arrived a century ago to put down a nationalist revolt and stayed for twenty years. Soon we were at the guesthouse, a half-dozen blocks from the six-storied Hilton and Intercontinental hotels, structural anomalies in this earthquake-ravaged city. Set between two crater lakes, named Managua and Nicaragua, and beneath a multi-headed range of volcanoes, the city of Managua was last shaken to rubble in 1972 in one of the most chronicled seismic nightmares in modern times.

From the guesthouse desk I called one of my wife's colleagues who had promised to find Cowboy and me an English-speaking student interested in making some extra cash as a guide in Managua and to travel with us to Leon. An hour later, Erwin Arauz arrived.

Twenty-six years old, six feet tall, dark-skinned, slow-talking, with a hint of a U.S. southern accent (he probably learned his English by tape from a Texas teacher), Erwin had just finished a master's degree in business at Managua's Central American University. His mother was a school teacher, his father the business manager of a medical NGO. Erwin, gifted with a well-stocked mind and many talents, sang in the national choir, a gig that afforded him the opportunity to meet presidents and diplomats alike. Erwin's most noticeable attribute was that he had a calm and patience about him that went to his bones. He told us he led a clean life—no smoking, drinking, cussing, wild women or immoderate behavior—but owned up to being a self-professed jive-talking, dancing fool.

Most of that conduct was the result of his unique religion. Erwin was a fourth-generation follower of the Baha'i faith. Baha'is believe in one god, with a universe of messengers, Krishna, Buddha, Zoroaster, Abraham, Moses, Jesus, Mohammed. The founder, or Promised One, Baha'u'llah, also known as Bab, Erwin told us, was from Shiraz, Iran (formerly Persia). He died in Palestine where he had been imprisoned before being exiled after many followers were executed in Persia. Baha'is were mostly found in the Middle East until after Bab's death in 1892. They have now spread all over Asia, Africa, Europe, the U.S. and Latin America. Today, there are 2,000 adherents in Nicaragua and six million worldwide. The central tenets of Bab's teachings stress the importance of eliminating poverty, of harmony between religion and science, of peace, justice and unity among world religions. Other than the prohibitions on smoking, drinking and cussing, it seemed to me that one would have to be against mother's milk to dismiss Erwin's religion.

Cowboy, who was searching for more than gaucho hats and business deals, and at the time was reading a book titled *Understanding Women*, warmed to the idea that Erwin's Baha'i faith covered all the bases. In pursuit of that truth, Cowboy vetted Erwin for the next two days with questions like: Do you go to hell if you have more than one girlfriend? How do you have the time to read the Bible, Koran and all that Buddha stuff? Who's in charge when you go to church? Erwin answered the best he could.

"We pray directly to one god, there are no images, no temple, no preacher, only a coordinator and a house, where we go and say prayers and discuss Baha'i teachings," Edwin explained, as if informing two new acolytes. (Later he would take us to the Baha'i meeting house.) "If you break the rules [sin] and other members find out, they will call you out on it," he continued. "We are a close group. By way of example, if I go to New York, upon arrival, I can call a stranger who is a Baha'i, and he will pick me up at the airport and give me a place to stay. Trust is automatic."

Erwin told us about the evangelicals who often knock on his door. When he tells them that he reads the Bible and believes in Jesus, they press him to come to their church. "But when they find out that I am Baha'i and don't go to church," he said, "they say, 'No, you are the devil.' They don't like such a universal belief system." For what it's worth, Erwin was one of the nicest, most reflective and sensible (if not a little on the strait-laced side) young men that I had ever met.

❂ ❂ ❂

The next morning Cowboy was behind the wheel of our Toyota rental car. We had traveled only a few blocks when he downshifted, rounded a wide turn onto an open stretch, and shot off like a bat out of hell, headed for Leon, the former liberal capital of Nicaragua, spiritual home of the Sandinistas and historical rival to the more conservative city Granada.

Seconds after that turnoff, about the time Cowboy got those RPMs posted, three blue-uniformed, pot-bellied policemen appeared with a radar gun, waving us over. Erwin was nervous. He had never been stopped by cops, and his only reference for such an experience was 1985 when Sandinista police told his dad to get in a paddy wagon that they had already packed sardine-full. With no room, the police let him go that night. Cowboy was still in a hurry, proposing that we donate $100 to this police tollgate and move on. Instead, we agreed on $20 and appointed Erwin the spokesman and bag man for the stack of Nicaraguan Cordoba-equivalent.

"They are American tourists who just arrived…they are very sorry," Erwin explained, softening them up like a pro, then handing over the bribe, which the senior pot-belly buried in his hip pockets lickety-split. They motioned us ahead, waving goodbye. "That was easy," Erwin said, as he slid into the back seat, at once buoyed and befouled by all the neat things he was learning from his new gringo friends.

Off Cowboy went again, pedal back to the metal, swerving around chicken buses and horse-drawn carts that were more plentiful than cars. We barreled around a beautifully sculpted volcano set against the sea-like breadth of Lake Managua as if we were on the Indie 500 track. Slowing Cowboy down was next to impossible. "Put a halter on it," I'd say from the back seat, but Cowboy went one speed only—flat-out—exerting his gaucho right to go fast. Lucky for Ervin and I, though, a line of horse farms slowed Cowboy down and got him interested in the scenery. From those horse farms to Leon he and Erwin jawed about Nicaragua's equestrian history.

❂ ❂ ❂

Leon, Nicaragua's second largest city, is a living history of striking colonial architecture and faded elegance. A university town, Leon was traditionally considered an intellectual hotbed. Traveler, bon vivant, diplomat, and influential poet Ruben Dario, one of the country's two most revered figures, is native to Leon. He is buried in the main chapel of the Cathedral of the Assumption of Mary, the largest of its kind in Central America, setting center stage in the plaza. Though he is heralded as the father of modernist Spanish literature, *Latinos* love a fated man. Throughout his life he had many celebrated lovers but lived a life of unrequited love, which inspired much of his poetry. In later years, Dario became fixated on mysticism and morbidity (two daughters died), before he drank himself to death at age forty-nine, bankrupt and broken.

Today, the fabled poet is honored with statues, festivals, streets and buildings named for him; his poetry is remembered worldwide, along with his pan-Latin-American zeal. Though generally non-political, his poem *To Roosevelt* was written a few years after the Spanish-American War in response to President Theodore Roosevelt's bullying and support of the 1903 revolution in Panama that set the stage for the U.S. construction of the Panama Canal. A few spirited lines, including the closing ones that capture the poet's message:

> ...The United States is grand and powerful.
> Whenever it trembles, a profound shudder
> runs down the enormous backbone of the Andes.
> If it shouts, the sound is like the roar of a lion...

> ...It would take, Roosevelt, to be God himself,
> the terrible Rifleman and the strong Hunter,
> to be able to have us in his claws.

> And, since you have everything, one thing is missing:
> God!

148

❂ ❂ ❂

Another locally celebrated Nicaraguan hero is General Augusto Sandino, from whom the Sandinista National Liberation Front (SNLF) took its name. In the late '20s and early '30s, Sandino and his guerilla army carried on a six-year war with American Marines and the Nicaraguan National Guard. During that time, like Che and Castro and countless other anti-American guerrilla fighters of the 20th century, Mexico gave Sandino asylum for long intervals, seeking to limit American power as it has done ever since the lopsided Mexican-American War.

By 1933, after an occupation that lasted twenty years, American forces departed Nicaragua under the aegis of the "Good Neighbor Policy." General Sandino and his men surrendered their arms, gave support to the new regime, and were granted amnesty. Under the orders of National Guard General Anastasia Somoza, however, Sandino was ambushed, captured and taken to Managua where he was executed. Somoza would later claim he did so "with approval from U.S. Minister Arthur Bliss Lane."

Somoza and his family, American surrogates, would rule Nicaragua like a personal fiefdom for the next four decades, amassing a fortune and owning up to twenty percent of the land in Nicaragua. President Franklin Roosevelt was reputed to have quipped about the ruthless dictator, "Somoza may be a son of a bitch, but he's our son of a bitch."

Turnabout is fair play in the radical hotbed of Leon. In 1956, a poet (not Dario) gunned down Anastasia Somoza, who died several days later. Somoza's two sons succeeded him: Luis, who graduated from Louisiana State University, took over the presidential palace, while Anastasio Jr., who graduated from West Point, seized control of the military. With the American Embassy next door to the palace, where torture and killings were as common as dinner parties, the Yankee-dictator bond grew closer, not least because of the economic dependency that had evolved.

149

In 1958, Vice President Richard Nixon and his wife Pat made an eight-country Latin America tour. Luis Somoza was the only leader to show warmth in welcoming America's second couple. Nixon was spat upon in Caracas and almost thrashed by angry mobs. According to Cold War historian Walter LaFeber, Venezuelans were upset by a recent award given by Eisenhower to a dictator they had just overthrown. This should have given a hint of the rising anger south of the border.

❂ ❂ ❂

Ervin, Cowboy, and I took chairs outside at El Sesteo on the Plaza Parque Central de Leon, ordered plates of the local favorite, cabbage, fried pork and yucca, getting a taste of Leon. Postcard boys sold us black and white revolutionary photos of General Augusto Sandino, who struck a Pancho Villa pose, wearing a Stetson and wrapped in bandoleers; and of a young Sandinista girl with an AK-47 slung over her right shoulder and a baby suckling on her left breast. Brandishing a wide smile that verged on a laugh, the mother-cum-guerilla was either crowing about a victory or grinning at the absurd reality of it all.

But those were the old days. Erwin told us that when Violeta Chamorro, the first Latin woman head of state, was elected president in 1990, unseating Sandinista leader Daniel Ortega with a coalition government, she began her tenure by saying, "Give me your guns and I will give you land." It worked. Their AKs are now buried in concrete, and the new gun law imposes a two-year jail sentence for anyone caught with an unregistered weapon. The volatile problem of inequitable property ownership was, for the moment, tamped down. "They got rid of the guns, but there are still minefields in the north where the worst poverty exists," Erwin added.

Leon remains the spiritual heart of the Sandinistas. Everything there speaks revolution, a microcosm of Havana. Children are named for Marx and Lenin, and Castro's successors continue to provide doctors and medical assistance. On the sidewalks market ladies sell jocote, a bitter fruit eaten with salt, next to piles of page-worn books about the pantheon of Sandinista heroes, Marx, Lenin, Stalin, Castro, Che, with no other choices but for a text on geometry or the scientific tables. Vividly painted murals on pastel-colored buildings animated the streets, depicting the Somoza National Guard brought to heel in Goya-like spectral images as merchants of death, and beret-clad Sandinistas as heroes and martyrs. It's not hard to imagine the Cold War days when loudspeakers blasted the Sandinista anthem, "We fight against the Yankee, enemy of mankind." The specter of U.S. interventions will for the foreseeable future be part of the Nic psyche, as will the colonial aftershocks that fracture the region, and not just for Sandinistas.

Erwin told us about life in Nicaragua during the 1980s civil war. "Everyone wanted the revolution but no one foresaw how it would turn out," he said. "There was no meat, sugar, milk or tissue paper for most. Rice was rationed at one pound a week per person. My uncle was caught with extra rice under the Sandinistas and was taken away and threatened with death. Revolutionaries are never good administrators."

During the civil war, one U.S. observer quipped that your average American cat was fed more meat than most Nics. What Erwin didn't mention were the CIA-directed bombings of Leon and Managua, the mining of Nicaragua's harbors, and the political and economic blockades (over 200 million in development loans), orchestrated by single-minded and often unscrupulous Cold War schemers, not the least being CIA Director William Casey and National Security staffer Oliver North.

❂ ❂ ❂

Lost in reverie there on the sidewalk in Leon, my mind drifted back to another lifetime when I was a C.P.A. and CFO of an oil and gas company. It was May of 1986 at the Opryland Hotel, located near Nashville, Tennessee. At a morning plenary session of the annual

IPAA (Independent Petroleum Association of America) meeting, in a packed room of over a thousand, attended by some of the wealthiest and most conservative people in America, while getting coffee I bumped into the featured speaker, Lieutenant Colonel Oliver North. We shook hands and I told him I also had the Vietnam Campaign and Service medals, which he was wearing on his dress uniform along with six rows of chest candy. He smiled, said nice to meet you, and that was it. He had a lot more to say, however, to the packed room. Purportedly speaking on behalf of "The National Endowment for the Preservation of Liberty," for the next hour he presented a slide show of the civil war, giving total attention to the atrocities suffered by the Contras. For most of the conservative-minded Reaganites there at the Opryland, all this was a hallelujah-and-hand-over-the-heart moment. My gut instinct, on the other hand, almost always lands me on the side of the underdog. In this case, North came off as articulate, sincere, and sympathetic, but it turned out that almost everything he said that day was based on lies and deceit.

Wearing the army dress uniform and all that chest candy, he understood that he was representing the United States. He had full knowledge that the Boland Amendment prohibited funding to the Contras, yet after his presentation North made solicitations to the audience of deep pockets. That event and the name of Oliver North might have slipped my mind forever, but less than six months later the Iran-Contra affair story broke. It was soon revealed that the National Endowment for the Preservation of Liberty was a shell company, a total fraud. North not only had been doing his dirty little solicitations, he had been selling arms (with Israel as the intermediary) to America's number one enemy, Iran, overcharging them by as much as 600 percent, and 'skimming the profits' to purchase weapons for the Nicaragua Contras. Drug kingpin and Panamanian dictator Manuel Noriega helped him funnel the weapons to the Contras. Under oath, 'America's favorite gung ho marine called the scam a *neat idea.*'

The confluence of shady events, by some conspiracy of fate, that brought Iran and Nicaragua together as partners in an illegal, duplicitous U.S. arms deal is too rich with irony. Only five years before, in 1979, both countries had gone through mass-based, anti-American revolutions that overthrew long-serving Yankee-backed dictators, the Somozas for forty-three years in Nicaragua and the Shah for twenty-five years in Iran.

❂ ❂ ❂

A row of beauty queens, creatures of uncommon human clay, all in hot pants or tight blue jeans with long-lashed eyes, pranced by like loons preening and shaking and took their place in the sun on the steps of the Cathedral of the Assumption of Mary between two guardian lions. Each of them was adorned in a white banner emblazoned in royal blue, with names like Daniela and Christiana spread across their chests. According to Erwin, they were there for photo ops for the Lent season carnival pageant.

With that bit of information, we buzzed off from our shaded table like drones to honey, snapping photos as if on assignment, shadowing the beauty queens, a single file of rolling rear ends, right into the cathedral. First, they posed in front of the Virgin Mary, followed by ablutions at a nearby fountain. They then sashayed like a chorus line over to Ruben Dario's crypt, which is crested by a sculpted lion and aptly inscribed with "Nicaragua is created of vigor and glory, Nicaragua is made for Freedom." Latin Americans regard their beauty contest winners with esteem, often conferring on them not just celebrity status but diplomatic and political power. We aging gringos, and a growing mass of the beguiled, too, felt their gravitas.

Bang, Bang, Bang, fireworks blasted in Chinese profusion around the plaza. A local politician was getting married in the side chapel to the Cathedral. Tuxedoed and smartly dressed friends and relatives gathered. We walked around the wedding party to the steamy market, laden with heaps of fresh produce, textiles from the

Taiwanese factory in Managua that employs 50,000 locals, and American CDs and DVDs. A crowd had gathered. We were among a sea of brown eyes and dark luminous bodies, lean men and bare-shouldered women, displaying the alegria they are famous for.

Erwin talked about "the invasion of American culture" in Nicaragua with the middle class of his generation. "The U.S., not Europe or South America, is our point of reference," he said. "American brands, Levi, Hilfiger, Klein, big jeans, flat hats and base-ball caps, Atlantic coast R&B, hip hop, the Titanic, Matrix, Superman, MTV, are what we like. People I know dress like 50 Cent; it's almost like a uniform. Most of my friends drink alcohol but don't do drugs. We go to clubs, arrive in a car with the music turned up, the windows down; everyone sees you at the entrance. It's cool."

In the early evening we drove to a military redoubt outside of Leon, where, in 1979, the Somoza National Guard made their last stand before falling to the Sandinistas. Moments before cresting the hill to the fort, we had to pass through a smoldering dump where turkey buzzards, cows, horses and human scavengers all sniffed among the refuse. The semi-circle of bunkers, overlooking Leon and the valley, are now abandoned. Other than graffiti and bullet-riddled concrete there is no memorial. It was all symbolic of the American attention span. In the late '70s and '80s, wresting Nicaragua from Daniel Ortega and the Sandinistas was critical to free world stability.

❂ ❂ ❂

The next morning, we followed a horse-drawn funeral cortege into Granada, the oldest continuously inhabited city in the Americas. Erwin said only important people can afford such funeral expense. In this case, we were witnessing the funeral of the black-and-white-liveried driver, known as El Conejo, or the Rabbit, who was, according to Erwin, by the nature of his trade fast with the women. A crowd of mourners, hoisting umbrellas for protection from the sun, followed the dark mahogany-paneled hearse, blanketed in wreaths. As they turned off toward the cemetery we parked next to the market.

If Leon was poor and liberal, Granada was conservative and middle-class to wealthy. Their rivalry is a tale of two cities, of the powerful and powerless, who fought against each other for two centuries, intensely so after independence in the 1820s, until Managua, located in the geographic middle, was made the capital in a moment of compromise.

Today, the old city of Granada has the same charm as Antigua, Guatemala, with a tumultuous history to go with it. Pastel-painted stucco buildings, with courtyards hidden behind tall wooden doors, are the homes, guesthouses, bars and restaurants, serving up everything from barbecue and lake bass to traditional fare and French cuisine. Horse-drawn carriages, festooned with yellow, lavender and powder blue ribbons, clop-clopped around the cobble-stoned central plaza, Parque Colon. Spirited marimba players and castanet dancers livened up the streets. Rimmed by red flame trees, bulbous mangoes and skinny, windblown palms, food kiosks stood on every corner.

Art galleries featured dancing figures and horse-face images of "El Gueguense," the quintessential, satirical Nicaraguan play that spoofs the Spanish conquerors for rising to aristocracy through deceptive means. The play features folkloric dancing and easy melodies thought to be passed on from 16th century Indians and mestizos. During Granada's many festivals the play is performed in local theaters.

On the south side of Granada, planted in coffee and corn, the fertile slopes of Mombacho Volcano climbed skyways. Only a few blocks to the east are the lush shores of Lake Nicaragua, teeming with tarpon and sharks. The crater lake is connected by the San Juan River to the Caribbean, once making Granada vulnerable to French and English buccaneer attacks (if not others).

Erwin showed us around Casa de los Leones, now a museum and gallery and rebuilt to its former 1920s glory. In 1856, members of William Walker's army torched the original Casa, along with most of Granada's 16th century buildings, leaving behind a message in the ruins, "Granada was here."

❂ ❂ ❂

William Walker is little known in American history, but has rock star notoriety in Nicaragua, Honduras and Costa Rica. The American freebooter, known as *filibustero* during the pirate days of the colonial-era Caribbean, once worked in the service of Yankee super-capitalist Cornelius Vanderbilt's Accessory Transit Company. During the days of the California gold rush, the Company shipped people and provisions from New York to San Francisco via the isthmus of Nicaragua.

In the 1850s, as civil war overtook Nicaragua, Walker struck a deal with Leon's Liberal opposition party to muster a mercenary army of "colonists" to seize power from the conservatives of Granada. Recruits included fewer than a hundred Americans, three Europeans, and a few dozen locals. In short order, Walker's ragtag expeditionary force defeated the national army in Riva, a farming village on Vanderbilt's transit route to the Pacific. From there the mercenaries subdued Granada, the capital, giving Walker effective control of the military and the country. On May 20, 1856, he declared himself president of Nicaragua, and English became the state language. U.S. President Franklin Pierce extended diplomatic recognition to Walker.

In Walker's abrupt rise to monarchal power, he had double-crossed Vanderbilt, cutting him out of his local steamship business. Realizing the hammer was getting ready to fall, Walker switched strategies and appealed to fellow Southerners (he was born in Nashville) to rally behind him to make Central America a slave-owning extension of the South, quite a turnaround given that he came to Nicaragua to save the liberal, poor people of Leon. Meanwhile, Vanderbilt wasn't tolerating Walker's betrayal. He convinced the powers that be in Washington to recant its blessing and then financed an army of Central Americans to bring the filibustero to heel.

Walker managed to avoid capture by the Central American army, surrendered to American forces and returned to the States by U.S. navy ship to a short-lived hero's welcome in New York City. At his core Walker was a pirate and the American North was anti-slavery. In 1860, as tensions escalated between abolitionist Northerners and slave-holding Southerners, ever restless, Walker returned to Central America. Upon landing on the northern shores of Honduras, the British navy, who saw him as disruptive to their trade interests in the region, arrested him and turned him over to the Honduran army. Walker, who was known by his followers as "the grey-eyed man of destiny," was executed by firing squad in Trujillo, where he is buried.

Late in the afternoon we approached Rivas, where Walker had surrendered to Americans. No memorial marked the historic arrest. We were surrounded by plantations of bananas, coffee, and corn, along with orchards of jocote, all fields of plenty. Women sat beneath palapas selling melons, sugarcane and jocote. We pushed on south, down crumbling tracks of asphalt, to San Juan del Sur, the port city where Vanderbilt's steamships once loaded and unloaded. In that era, this slice of the isthmus was considered the more viable option for a canal connecting the Atlantic and Pacific, which Walker planned to build with his Central American slaves. Even today, over a century and a half later, the idea of building a canal here is seen as a way of bringing long-term commercial exuberance to Nicaragua.

As we arrived, a tangerine sunset fell over the horseshoe-shaped harbor. Near the same freight docks that might have originally been Vanderbilt's, among a quaint scattering of fishing skiffs, a Windstar Cruise ship docked in the blue waters was as out of character to my newly-arrived sensibility as a protean monster. There was no night life, designer clothes shopping or high–end crafts market to keep the passengers' interest, so they descended upon the fishing village, hailing taxis to Granada. On the other hand, surfers, from everywhere, frequent San Juan del Sur, make their own fun at night, and take off to the northern beaches by day.

❂ ❂ ❂

Erwin and I were checking out the rooms at a modest surfer guesthouse in the village center when Cowboy arrived, panting, saying, "I've been looking everywhere for you guys." He had rented a condo at Pelican Eyes, a posh retreat atop the hill overlooking the harbor, at a cost of a year's income for those back in Morocopay, Honduras. Once there, it seemed vulgar, with its three infinity pools and uniformed lickspittles in pressed and pleated shirts, matching shorts and white socks, trained to kiss every arrival's ass. We had checked out of Nicaragua and into Fantasy Island. Erwin's eyes popped from his head as he inspected the three-bedroom condo with a view of the world. He turned on the cable TV, grabbed a liter bottle of Coke and bag of chips we had picked up at the local tienda, and hardly left the couch for two days.

In the village, Coldwell Banker and RE/MAX signs were everywhere. Waterfront lots were selling for $100,000, and Pelican Eyes condos were going for somewhere between $275,000 and $600,000, depending on whom you were talking to. Cowboy took a brochure and talked up buying one. Tax incentives, low crime rates, and the cheap alternative to the half-a-million-dollar starting prices for condos in Costa Rica were added selling points. Tourism in San Juan del Sur, with up to 800,000 visitors annually, mostly Costa Ricans but also several thousand Americans, is the top source of hard currency for the picturesque coastal town.

In Managua, only a few days before, President Chavez of Venezuela, had blustered about the "socialist revolution" and about "internal adversaries" supported by the U.S. who would try to stop the revolution. The newly-resurrected President Daniel Ortega had a delicate balance to strike between his patron and ideological soul mate and his Cold War nemesis, prospective investor and provider of development money, the United States. Still in the first 100 days of his new administration, everyone, including the owners of Pelican Eyes, were nervous about what Ortega would do next. "It's a given that thirty-eight percent of the vote is not exactly a mandate, with no other party having more than twenty-eight percent representation in parliament," said George Knight, one of the original investors in Pelican Eyes we met in the lobby. "If he runs the investors off, they won't come back. The government has no other money." (In July of 2025, according to their online reservation system, Pelican Eyes was fully booked. Condo prices were flat, the same range as they were on my visit.)

Third World Playboys and the Panama Canal

Chapter Seven

IN MANAGUA, TWO DAYS LATER, the pulquerias were all barred shut. Even the dogs had stopped barking as Cowboy and I walked several blocks to the Tica bus station, watching the sun rise over the sleepy city. The six o'clock bus we boarded was packed with Costa Ricans returning home from holiday, and Nicaraguans leaving home and going back to work in Costa Rica. As we traced the western shores of Lake Nicaragua, next to me sat a twenty-two-year-old American student from San Diego who had been partying down with the surfers in San Juan del Sur. "It depends on how you carry yourself here," she said. "If you try to speak the language, they accept you. If you treat it like your playground, you're the ugly American." I was unsure if she was talking about me, herself, Cowboy or someone else.

At the border there was a veritable sucking noise of Nicaraguans migrating south to Costa Rica, a sharp demarcation between haves and have nots, much like the northern flow from Mexico to the U.S. The visa lines were long and as steamy as a Turkish bath, but there was a secondary system: for a $10 bribe, hustlers would expedite the paperwork. That meant going ahead of everyone waiting in front of us, most of whom couldn't afford the tariff. I chose not to be that guy, but I've never seen an Alexander Hamilton given up so quickly as Cowboy did. He bolted from the line and spent the next three hours in front of a fan, eating fried chicken and ice cream and drinking Cokes. Thing was the bus wasn't leaving until we all got stamped out and in.

Lucas, six-foot-five, a pure Californian, sun-bleached, shirtless, scary-haired, sandaled, and wearing flowered trunks stood in front of me. He was about my age, with a highly dubious résumé. A land-owning-resident of Costa Rica on a visa run, a Vietnam combat Vet, a former Peace Corps volunteer in Haiti, and an ex-resident of a homeless shelter in San Diego. Zelig at large or not, it didn't matter if any of it was true, Lucas was a laugh a minute, rat-a-tat-tat. When four Boy-Scout-looking Canadians marched up with the same back-packs, all with hiking garments from Mountain Equipment Co-op, asking about logistics, off Lucas went on their maple leaves: "Don't talk to us, we're Americans! They're going to kidnap us if you don't turn over your maple leaves. Better move on, quick, quick, quick, they might take you too."

The Canadians' bewildered expressions seemed to suggest, *You gringos are frigging mad!*

"Where you guys been?" Cowboy asked, all cool and refreshed, talking to others waiting on the Tica bus, working on his second ice cream cone. Before long we were back on the bus, the gabfest with Lucas over. Grinding the gears through the border town of Penas Blancas, we turned onto the most well-kept stretch of the Pan American Highway we'd seen since we were north of Oaxaca, Mexico. Wending through the Guanacaste Mountains, hillsides of coffee grew in profusion next to large tracts of reforested farms and public land. Third World techno flowers—the discarded pink and powder-blue plastic bags that garnish the roadsides throughout Central America—were nowhere to be seen. Costa Rica is a different kind of place: twenty-five percent of the country has been designated either a national park or protected area.

At the border, I had picked up a copy of the Tico *Times*, the daily English language newspaper. There was lots of news: Nicaragua's ministry of tourism was holding an investment conference in San Jose; Queen Noor of Jordan was in Santa Ana for the inauguration of a newly opened United World College, a bilingual university program attended by students from sixty-four countries; and the Central American Free Trade Agreement (CAFTA) was the focus of street protests and national assembly debates. Ticos, as locals are called, were raising questions about sovereignty, about giving corporations parity with national governments, about runaway development, and about turning the country into more of a playground for foreigners than it already is.

Costa Rica, which means "rich coast," has marched to its own beat since the arrival of the Spanish. In spite of the name given by Christopher Columbus in 1502 on his fourth New World journey, there were no significant deposits of gold in Costa Rica. It was worn as jewelry by the coastal tribes Columbus encountered, but gold was prized by the Indians because of its scarcity. Once the conquerors either moved the Indigenes out, or they died from disease or were bred into a predominantly Creole population, Ticos were blissfully ignored by the Spanish colonists. The irony is that it was their "poverty," in the eyes of the Spanish, which today makes Costa Rica the wealthiest, least conflict and class-ridden country in Central America. In 1821, when the captaincy of Guatemala declared Central America independent of Spanish rule, Ticos were uninspired.

Over the 20th century, and into the 21st, Costa Rica has proven to be the most stable democracy in Central America. It constitutionally abolished its army sixty years ago, but on several occasions since the U.S. has pressured the government to militarize. For example, during the '80s, with Costa Rica's economy faltering from low coffee and banana prices and high public debt, the U.S. turned the screws, offering up debt relief and a substantial increase in foreign aid to get the Tico government off the fence and on the side of the Contras. Soon, American Green Berets arrived to turn the Civil Guard into more of an army than a police force; then the CIA built a secret landing strip to help supply the Contras. The Ticos' unwarlike history, their tribal distaste for Nics and all their overflowing conflicts, not least the 200,000 refugees that had crossed the border, had left Costa Rica reluctant to extend their involvement much further. When the public found out about the secret landing strip, street protests erupted.

Jose Figueres, a national hero and three-time president, whose terms in office spanned thirty years, oversaw the constitutional abolition of the army, voted on by an elected assembly. At the same time women and illiterates were empowered with the right to vote, a state welfare system was established, and banks were nationalized.

Once civil unrest in Costa Rica ended, Figueres stepped down. Free elections were held for the first time in 1953 and have been ever since. That for decades Costa Rica was the only Central American country that was not a dictatorship turned Figueres into an outspoken critic of military autocrats, particularly of the U.S.-backed Somoza regime in neighboring Nicaragua. His successors, for the most part, offered up a Swiss-like neutrality.

Not surprisingly, Costa Rican President Oscar Arias Sanchez won a Nobel Peace Prize in 1987 for forging a peace agreement among Central American nations that called for putting down arms and holding free elections. American President Ronald Reagan fought the peace agreement tooth and nail, but in the end Arias's plan worked. In 1990, the Sandinistas and Ortega left power peacefully after losing a fair election. As one observer noted, the only city the Contras ever took during the civil war was Washington D.C.

It has been peace and economic development that has underpinned Costa Rica's success as a progressive-minded country. Figueres once called the Costa Rican political experience "a deeper and more human revolution than that of Cuba."

It's that human revolution, and the stability that came with it, that has attracted companies like Intel, who recognized the availability of an educated work force, particularly in STEM fields, that could provide the necessary engineers and production staff for an assembly plant. Today, Costa Rica is a tech hub: Microchip processors and medical devices account for almost twenty-five percent of exports.

It is little wonder that a million North Americans travel to Costa Rica each year, while tens of thousands have chosen the country's gated communities of condos on prime beachfront and hillside properties for retirement. The U.S. dollar delivers bargains in Costa Rica.

❂ ❂ ❂

As we arrived in San Jose early in the afternoon, an American retiree on the bus gave us a tip on an inexpensive, walkup hotel off the National Plaza of Culture, a ten-block walk from the bus station. Along the way billboards warned against pedophilia, something I had not seen during my past visits to Costa Rica. The plaza was full of tourists and Tico couples sitting on park benches, feeding hungry pigeons, surrounded by designer shops and the stately Pre-Columbian and Gold Museum, where one of the largest collections of gold artifacts in the Americas is housed. It's amazing that there was any gold left to display. I would soon learn that the Spanish robbed graves and shook down the living, on an imperial mission to melt into bullion every existing funerary figurine of crocodiles, birds, jaguars, frogs, turtles, deer, armadillo, hummingbirds, lobster, crab and shrimp, all artwork that was reflective of the Indigenes' environment in Costa Rica at the time.

While Cowboy found a barber shop, I walked two blocks to the National Park, shaded by tall cedars and laurels. In the center of the park, atop a cylindrical concrete pedestal, was a bronze statue, depicting a dynamic scene of fighting men. While taking in the statue, I was approached by a diminutive, Chaplinesque man, wearing a blue undertaker's tie, a rumpled black suit, and thick, taped glasses.

164

"Hi, I'm Carlito. We were kicking some ass up there," he said, with a puckish wit about him. He then pointed to the monument where my stare was fixed and said in a matter-of-fact tone: "You are from America, home of the free and land of the brave. We Costa Ricans are known as lovers, not fighters." For a negotiated guide fee of two dollars, Carlito then unraveled the story of the Iwo Jima-like shrine.

One of the half-a-dozen fighting men who were armed with swords and chasing a single man away was Juan Santamaria, a drummer boy from Alajuela. The date was April 11, 1856. The man being chased was the aforementioned American freebooter, William Walker. His rag-tag army had been defeated by Tico forces at the battle of Santa Rosa. From there Juan Santamaria and fellow Tico fighters pursued Walker on to Rivas, in Nicaragua. Once in Rivas, Santamaria torched the building where Walker was holed up, forcing him to flee again. Walker survived that day, but Santamaria was killed, and is now lionized throughout Costa Rica. Chasing a Yankee imperialist out of the country became an enduring symbol of Tico nationalism.

Before leaving, Carlito gave me a card for the New Fantasy massage parlor, saying, "We are now like Thailand, you know. But these are good college-age Catholic girls, they repent on Sunday and then it's okay."

Early that evening Cowboy and I treated ourselves to a steak dinner at the Café Del Rey, American-owned and said to have mafia connections. The Del Rey complex of buildings, which included a casino and hotel, is located between the Plaza of Culture and Congress Hall. It was only six o'clock, and the ballroom-sized restaurant was empty but for us. Once finished with the New York strips and girded by a few Imperial lagers, we ventured across the street to the Blue Marlin bar in the Del Rey Hotel, a neo-classic pink pleasure palace. At the entrance, a gauntlet of hustlers, including Carlito, who was now passing out cards for a strip club, greeted us with offers of cocaine, Cohibas, and cheap sex.

Inside, it was surreal. The clientele looked to be a gathering of the AARP, all between fifty and eighty years old, wearing patriotic hats and weighing on average above 200 pounds. That's it, they were fat, older Americans, grandpas and great-grandpas. Next to the bar was a travel agency, offering day trips for marlin fishing, a bank of old IBM computers for internet access, and in the Blue Marlin, ESPN on flat screens.

But these were no mall-walking sports freaks. The Del Rey was a top-end brothel, and these AARP folks were sex tourists, Third World playboys. Here, you didn't have to be good at sport fishing to catch one. These waters were target rich. Whether bellied up at the bar, pulling on the one-arm bandits, or perched at the blackjack tables, most of the AARP crowd were accompanied by young cuties. And for the unescorted, a steady procession of provocatively-dressed sex workers filed through. Off subsistence farms, out of slums and im-poverished homes, the ladies of pleasure were from an atlas of coun-tries across Latin America and the Caribbean to Eastern Europe and Russia, casting their nets in this sinkhole of venery with come-hither eyes and smiles, or giving a playful, painted-nail scratch across the belly, saying, in their transactional, limited English, "You're the one." To our seniors, the Del Rey Hotel and Marlin Bar must have been the land of the mythical patriarch Prester John, the fountain of youth that Ponce de Leon once searched for (without success I might add).

❂ ❂ ❂

Two days later, at 5:30 in the morning, Cowboy and I were again busing down the Pan American Highway, crossing the Talamanca Mountains. The road was vastly better than when I had traveled through many years before. Then, the potholes and buckled pavement were so bad that we had two flats on the three-hour drive that turned into seven. On this day, along the fresh-sealed road the sub-tropical forest was lush with flame trees, vines and creepers, straight-as-a-string hardwoods, and epiphytes with canary yellow, magenta, and pink-to-red blooms. We even watched a yellow-billed toucan seemingly conduct us down the road. From forested ridge-lines stacked in billowy clouds, we fell into tumbling valleys, and by nine o'clock, into the highlands market town of San Isidro.

Almost two decades ago, on an extended Thanksgiving school holiday, my kids and I, and two friends and their children, had passed through San Isidro on our way to climb nearby Mt. Chirripo, the highest point in Costa Rica. On a clear day from Chirripo's peak, it's possible to see the Pacific and the Atlantic. We had far from a clear day, though, and hurried down the mountain rain soaked and dead on our feet. As trail boss of this pack of hound-dog-faced hikers, I immediately loaded them up in a beat-up Volkswagen van, and hit the highway in a surging downpour. A flat tire later, we arrived at the wildlife-rich Manuel Antonio National Park on the Pacific Coast. On a good day at Manuel Antonio we would have hiked game trails and spotted white-faced capuchin monkeys and three-toed sloths, but, due to the non-stop deluge, had to settle for a porch seat at the cabin and the company of a few resident iguanas. Upon our return to Arkansas, my kids threatened to turn me into the Department of Human Services for child abuse.

✪ ✪ ✪

On this day in San Isidro, Cowboy and I had to change buses, but the southbound depot was a few blocks away. By the time we got to the station, our connecting bus had just pulled out for Dominical. As luck seemed to have it, Miguel, a taxi-driver, told us to hop in his pasted-together vintage Toyota and he would catch the bus. Hastily, with language limitations, we agreed on a price and off we lurched, shimmying down the road, the Toyota's transmission all but gone. He had to downshift to first gear to get over the slightest incline. Thing was Miguel knew all along that we weren't going to overcome the rural bus: He was playing us for the twenty-five-mile ride to Dominical. Once his scam became obvious, we agreed on a new price. To make sure we understood each other, I wrote it down on the newspaper I was reading for him to see.

Two hours later, we chugged into the laidback, surfer paradise of Dominical. The bus we had missed was just pulling out. So, I quickly handed Miguel the money, while writhing out the passenger window because the door wouldn't open. Cowboy and I threw our bags in the bus's cargo hull, and the driver welcomed us. Miguel stormed up to the bus door, cursing and spitting. He threw the money at me, wheeled around and charged two doors down to the police station. Moments later, he returned with two officers of the law, who ordered us off the bus and back to the police station. By now surfers and locals had gathered to watch what had become a scene for gawkers. It wasn't even noon and we were being escorted into the police station, two guys in their late fifties, carrying dusty duffel-bags, with Cowboy wearing all camouflage. After a screaming match, I produced the newspaper with the amount we had agreed on written on the front page and circled. At that point, the police asked Miguel for his taxi license, which he didn't have. The argument was settled. Miguel ran out and we never saw him again.

Buoyed by our acquittal, I protested that we had just missed another bus to Ocha Jal, about ten miles down the road. The next one wouldn't be around for another four hours. It was oppressively hot, so walking along the asphalt was not our first choice. Soon, however, one of the policemen offered us a ride, saying he was going that direction anyway. When he dropped us on the highway near a property Cowboy had recently purchased, he demanded $20, which is what Miguel had asked us to pay. Lesson learned. Don't get in a hurry. Wait on the bus, be happy.

Ocha Jal is where rugged mountains, fast-moving streams, lush rainforest and the Pacific Ocean converge. A few years ago Cowboy had purchased a 200-acre property there. He kept four horses on a hill top where his farm manager, Roger, who was the son of the previous owner, and his wife lived in an old house with no indoor plumbing. Roger's dad retained forty acres and the big house. In our first two days in Ocha Jal, Cowboy hurried around, trying to hire a contractor to build a trestle bridge across a small river with crystal clear swimming holes.

In his mid-thirties, muscled up from a life of hard work, Roger had only a third-grade education. He and Rachel had no children. Cowboy speculated that Roger was sterile from spraying toxic chemicals for the neighboring cashew and palm oil farms since he was a kid. Be that as it may, Roger and Rachel smiled all the time, giddy in love, on a permanent honeymoon, heart strong people.

Roger knew the ecology on the property, the plant life, how to handle horses and how to swing a machete to cut vines, and clear a pathway of fallen timber. For two days he and I rode horses through the rainforest. The hothouse verdure was the same each day, lyrical in its larger-than-life novelty. Howler monkeys sounded with the lungs of lions, butterflies grew as big as birds, hardwoods spiraled to the clouds like pillars to heaven, tiny red ants stung with the might of wasps, yellow and black toucans showed themselves as freely as gulls above the open ocean, frogs were as colorful as coral fish, and the cicada cried and buzzed in a jarring cacophony that would quiet a sawmill. All the while, seeing the beauty in common things, Roger hacked away, then stopped and plucked a sausage-shaped fruit from a branch, diced it up, handed me a slice, and off we'd go, spitting out the seeds as if eating watermelon.

We were staying down the road from Cowboy's property at the Gaia Village, an assortment of scattered cottages, a few of which overlooked the ocean, in a stretch of tropical forest. Next door to the Gaia was Gringo Mike's, a large oceanfront house and guest cottage that rumor had it had just sold to an American neurosurgeon for 1.8 million dollars. Gringo Mike's had a nasty reputation around the village for shady business deals. Everyone was waiting to exhale.

169

The village of Ocha Jal has an odd mix of French-Canadians and Americans, some of whom arrived as investors in palm oil farms, and Tico subsistence farmers and laborers, living off the jobs that come their way from real estate development. The village center, anchored by a bullfighting ring now used for rodeos on festival days, lies at the end of a mile-long dirt track. Three or four real estate offices lined the Pan-American Highway. Above, steep, forested hillsides were slowly being shaved away for more high-end retirement homes. Developers would say things were booming. Word on the street had it that a new brothel, owned by an American, with mostly Colombian women, had just opened south of Ocha Jal at Palmar Norte, near the Panama border.

It's difficult to say whether the force of gravity that pulls poor migrants to the States for work is stronger than the juggernaut that compels investors to go in the opposite direction to exploit a bargain. They do seem to always cross paths, though, one way or the other.

Cowboy and I had dinner at Exotica, owned by a French-Canadian woman and maybe the only Ocha Jal restaurant open at night. The epicurean fixed menu consisted of a cognac pâte, smoked salmon, tuna with ginger and bananas flambé for dessert. An Israeli man and his la-di-da partner from Maryland, who boasted about his connections to fellow Arkansan, Bill Clinton, sat at the next table with two architects, working out plans for a condo development. Ticos served the food, but there were none dining. Joining us was an American contractor and his wife. We talked a lot that night about the bridge project, but after all was said, who knows what Cowboy will decide to do with his piece of tropical paradise. If I were a betting man, in five years the ancient rainforest will be scraped from the earth and replaced by condos. (Due to time constraints and a waning interest, Cowboy sold the property a few years later without building the bridge or making any other improvements.)

At five in the morning we blinked the lights of Cowboy's old jeep that he keeps on the farm at Roger and Rachel's house. An hour later we were crossing the border at Paso Canoas into Panama, saying goodbye to Roger and Rachel, who were going to spend the day in nearby Palmar Norte. With the help of a hustler, who, by dint of sheer persistence had insinuated himself and his services into our lives as a fixer, we went through the paces of immigration. A window over here for a five-dollar tourist card, a door over there for a dollar stamp on the card, and a visa stamp somewhere else. By chance the overnight Tica bus was parked by the immigration outpost, meaning we didn't have to take two or three local buses on to Panama City.

The Tica bus was packed to capacity. Two rows in front of a badly befouled toilet, I slid in next to an older Panamanian lady, who told me she was a retired school teacher. While I pulled out a book and read about New Spain and the Indian massacres, she read her Bible, Samuel 10:11-12, the Old Testament story of King David and Joab, his nephew and captain of his army, and Ammonites and Arameans squaring off in a "just" battle, killing at least 700 charioteers and 40,000-foot soldiers. Killing in the name of God, a hot topic on the home stretch.

We were horses smelling the barn, as Cowboy says, making time down the four-lane Pan American Highway…until the driver pulled off on the shoulder of the road in Santiago next to a police station. Four heavily-armed soldiers, wearing the PDF (Panama Defense Forces) insignia of Manual Noriega's former National Guard, boarded and checked everyone's passport. Twenty minutes later they escorted a Mexican man sitting behind me off the bus. He had told me he was on his way to see a girlfriend. He looked terrified. The school teacher glanced up from her Bible, and laconically said, "They always know who they are looking for." A half-hour later the man returned, visibly shaken but relieved. It had been a case of mistaken identity.

The driver pulled over for an early lunch stop. Standing in line at the truck stop I met a Spanish couple on a two-seat bicycle, the wheels covered in saddlebags. Outfitted like matching bumblebees in yellow and black cycling gear, they had started their trip in Morocco, rode across the Sahara to Senegal, flown to Brazil, and cycled from Rio to here, all of which had taken six months. From Panama they would take another year-and-a-half to travel north up the Pan American Highway and across the U.S. and Canada, before flying to China and pedaling from there on to Europe.

Their daring odyssey made our bus adventure seem like a walk in the park. They would pedal 25,000 miles, roughly the circumference of the globe, over two years; whereas we had traveled 2,800 miles on fifteen buses, four of them overnight rides, and mostly air-conditioned. At this point, we had been on the road almost seven weeks. While slurping up a bowl of chicken soup (*sancocho*), I shared a few travel stories of Asia and Africa with the intrepid Spaniards, until it was time to wave goodbye and board the bus one last time.

By mid-afternoon we were crossing the Gulf of Panama, the Pacific Ocean end of the Panama Canal, on the Bridge of the Americas, built with U.S. dollars in the late '50s. It was at the southern foot of this bridge that seething and armed Panamanian demonstrators gathered in 1962 to protest the U.S. government, police force and military in the Canal Zone. That protest set the stage for the bloody '64 riots, sparked by high school students who were determined to raise the flag of Panama at the Balboa High School in the Canal Zone. The students were responding to a prohibition order by the U.S. which only allowed the American flag to fly at the high school. Once the tear gas cleared and weapons were silenced, twenty-one Panamanians and four Americans were dead. With that, diplomatic relations between the two countries were suspended until 1977, at which time the Torrijos-Carter Treaty was signed, setting the stage

172

for the transfer of the canal to Panama. January 9th, the day the '64 riots began, is celebrated in Panama each year as Martyr's Day.

From our aerie on the cantilevered Bridge of the Americas, looking to the east, for forty-eight miles the inter-oceanic canal, one of the world's greatest engineering feats, runs through a series of locks, dams and sluice gates, across Lake Gatun to Colon and Limon Bay. Looking to the west was blue water and fifty or more anchored container ships, waiting for their pass through the canal. As far as the eye could see, fuel dumps, freighters and gantry cranes lined the fabled straits.

In 1996, Hutchison-Whampoa (now CK Hutchison), owned by Li Ka Shing, said to be the wealthiest man in China, won an international bid for a twenty-five-year contract to manage the operation of two of the five shipping ports—Balboa port on the Pacific side and Cristobal port on the Atlantic side. Foreign companies, including U.S. based ones, also manage the other ports. In 2025, BlackRock Inc. announced the acquisition of eighty percent of Hutchison Port Holdings. With 14,000 ships transiting each year, or an average of forty a day, maritime commerce is huge here. The U.S. is responsible for three-fourths of the cargo passing through the canal. Transit fees are charged by weight. A small craft pays as much as $67,000 for the ten-hour passage, whereas the larger container ships, those which are a snug fit for the *panamax* width of 33.5 meters, pay up to $240,000. With a railroad that transits from Balboa to Colon, freight is often offloaded from one ship and picked up on the other end by another.

❂ ❂ ❂

Soon, we were pulling into the humongous, modern central bus station, a former American airfield used for pilot training. No need to change money in Panama. Dollars worked just fine. We grabbed a taxi to a small hotel three blocks from the Veneto Hotel and Casino. High fences and iron grates protected the hotel in this quiet, El Cangrejo neighborhood, at least by day.

Back in Ocha Jal, Cowboy had lost one of the eight wide-brimmed hats he had bought along the way. Once we hit the streets in El Cangrejo he wondered aloud if he would have a chance to buy a hat in Panama. Well, he was in luck, white Panama hats were everywhere, coupled with a thriving trade in Stetsons, fedoras and custom-made leather wide brims. And there were two hatters across from the Veneto Hotel and Casino.

When the owner of one store saw Cowboy amble in, he remarked, "You walk like John Wayne." The smallish man then imitated the Duke, with his chest puffed out and legs bowed, as if on a horse, and hands open to the side, ready to draw. It wasn't until the engaging owner mentioned that there was a John Wayne village on some nearby island where the Duke had once stayed, with saloons, jails and wranglers, that Cowboy acknowledged him. A spirited discussion followed, but they never did pin down exactly where the Wild West Village was (or if it even existed).

An hour later, Cowboy bought two leather hats, bringing his new collection to nine. He then insisted that I have one as a payback for handling the bus logistics of the trip. Next thing I knew I was wearing a leather wide brim, with a Panama white straw hat wrapped in a black band, for a backup. From the store, Cowboy bee-lined back to the hotel and got in the shower with his new leather hats, soaked and stretched them to the size of his head, and then let them dry.

At the same time, I checked in at the casino to see about hiring a driver the next day. I stopped the floor manager with a question about directions and learned that her father had a car and took tourists to the canal and other historical sites.

It was dark by now. The neighborhood was ablaze in neon, the streets filling with the night crowd who were in mid-roar. In most places, I'm not sure what my physical aura evinces for locals, maybe deep-pocketed old fart, or unescorted fat foreigner or possibly just another random pedestrian. But in El Cangrejo I was roundly identified as a sex-deprived drug addict: I've never been offered sex and cocaine more anywhere I have traveled than on the three-block walk back to the hotel (read: I lived in Bangkok for two years).

Only two days before our arrival, a ship with Panama registry was busted near the Bridge of the Americas, with the largest payload in maritime history: 40,000 pounds of cocaine with an estimated street value of 500 million dollars. Enough Bolivian marching powder to keep Panama City and south Florida high till Kingdom Come.

❂ ❂ ❂

Horacio Dawkins, wearing a white flat cap, tennis shoes, jeans and a white shirt, waited outside the iron fence for us early the next morning. Of African descent, his family came from Barbados in the 1880s when the French were making a first failed attempt at developing the canal. He only started driving a taxi a few years ago after he lost his job as a mechanic at Cerveceria Nacional, the brewer of most of Panama's pale lager, with brands like Atlas and Balboa. "I started there at sixty cents an hour, and after twenty-eight years I was making $3.90 an hour," he told me. "What I miss most about working there is the five free beers they gave us each day."

We circled through the Plaza Cinco de Mayo and Horacio pointed out the hillside fence that separated Panama City from the park-like ex-Canal Zone once occupied by American forces. International critics of the occupation often compare the barrier of barbed wire, known locally as the "fence of shame," to the Berlin Wall. From there Horacio drove through the zone, around all the former stately homes of American officers, to training centers, headquarters buildings, and Balboa High School, the epicenter of the 1964 riots.

When I asked Horacio about the Americans leaving, he said, "I wish they were back. As a kid I used to shine boots for them and could make $12 a day. They put a lot of money in this economy." Turns out the economic impacts were significant: 4,000 jobs were lost when the Americans left, along with a multiplier effect that put two or three hundred million dollars a year into the economy.

The building of the Panama Canal brought coolies from Caribbean islands like Barbados, Martinique, Trinidad, Jamaica, and Guadeloupe. Rugged opportunists came from diverse countries such as China, Armenia, Spain, Greece, Italy, India, France, Colombia, Japan and the United States. Though mestizos make up sixty-five percent of Panama's three million people, these minority migrants, mostly of African descent, are now part of the tapestry that is Panama. "We don't have race problems here, just rich people with money saying stay away," Horacio said.

We drove from the ex-Canal Zone to the original Spanish city, Panama Viejo, founded in 1519, and torched by the notorious English brigand Henry Morgan in 1671. Next, it was across the causeway to Naos, Perico and the Flamenco Islands that once housed bunkers built by the U.S. army as a prison and later used by dictator Manuel Noriega for torture. All are now surrounded by yachts from Colombia and full of night life, bars and restaurants. Further along we passed through the barrios of Chorrera and San Miguel where residents had recently burned their own buildings. By Horacio's account, they continue to fire guns at each other from balcony to balcony, a worthy real-life model for Fortnite's Battle Royale.

We parked and walked the narrow streets of colonial Casco Antiguo. Indigenous Kuna women, wearing gold nose rings and traditional garments, deftly wove colorful textiles dockside where pirate and sugar plantation owner, Henry Morgan, had landed. Tattered laundry hung on paint-chipped, graffiti-stained buildings next to the stately Presidential Palace, the National Theater, and Independence Square, the scene of a celebration in 1903 when Panama seceded from Colombia. On this day a salsa band played in the plaza—after all famed musician Ruben Blades lives nearby. Down one narrow street women and children sat on front porches and picked the nits out of each other's hair. On the nearby beach, bare-chested men played volleyball and drank Balboa beer.

For a late lunch, we looked for a place along the oceanfront on Balboa Avenue. Close to the American Embassy, we passed a bronze statue commemorating Balboa, facing the Pacific with arms outstretched, as if to say, voila. The whole promenade smelled like a red tide had settled in. The Balboa statue is shadowed by a Hong Kong-like cluster of high rises, the center of Panama's thriving international banking business. With cab driver intuition, Horacio noted that they were owned by Israelis, Arabs and Chinese.

In the middle of it all was a new Colombian-owned mega-mall, where we parked and went in for lunch at Bennigan's. Seated by a window, we had an expansive view of the Pacific Ocean. And directly across the street was the Apostolic Nunciature, a small Catholic home for priests and the Holy See's Embassy in Panama. It's a nondescript, low-slung, fenced building, but in December of 1989 the eyes of the world were upon it. Dictator Manuel Noriega fled there when Operation Just Cause, an invasion force of 26,000 American troops, bore down on him.

By then Noriega had spent almost three decades working for the CIA. He was also thought to be feeding Castro and the Soviets information. Small wonder he had become America's enemy number one, a gangster at heart, profane, distrusting, and violent. His transgressions, aside from those for the CIA, included stealing elections, killing political enemies, closing down media who criticized him, and partnering with Colombian cartels on drug shipments to the U.S. But it was the killing of a single, unarmed American marine that precipitated the invasion that "left twenty-three U.S. soldiers and hundreds of civilians dead."

International law (and ethics) precluded the American army from breaking down the doors of a Vatican property. So instead, for several days the U.S. dispatched a helicopter to hover low over the priest's residence, creating intolerable noise levels, while also, with maximum decibel impact, blasting rock-'n-roll music backed up by the screaming rants of *The Howard Stern Show*. The military term for such interventions is PSYOPs, and on this occasion the plan was to drive everyone inside the residence bat shit crazy. But after complaints from the Vatican, they gave up the PSYOPs and waited Noriega out. The damage may have been done. Protests demanding Noriega's arrest spread across the city. With few options, the beleaguered dictator surrendered to Operation Just Cause. Whisked off to Miami, he was tried for drug trafficking and received a final sentence of thirty years in federal prison. Local papers reported that he was eligible for parole after eighteen years.

While having lunch, Horacio was reading all the speculative news about Noriega's upcoming release. "The blood is still fresh here. Noriega will not get off the plane alive," he said. His fears of the bloodthirsty dictator returning to power didn't come to pass. Noriega was released in the U.S. and tried for murder and corruption in Panama. He died in 2017 in Panama City while serving a life sentence in prison.

What's more, in the news was the current American enemy number one in Panama, Pedro Gonzalez, accused of opening fire on American soldiers during a 1992 visit by President George H.W. Bush. Gonzalez is alleged to have killed one of the soldiers because he was upset at Bush for Operation Just Cause. But Gonzalez is no ordinary fugitive. In 1997, he was tried in Panama courts and found not guilty of the crime. A few months after we were in Panama City, Gonzalez's status was elevated from being an elected legislator to the presidency of Panama's legislature—wanted and hated by America and loved and empowered by Panamanians.

✪ ✪ ✪

While in Panama Cowboy and I had hoped to take one of the day-long boat trips through the canal, from ocean to ocean. To our dismay, those boats are booked well in advance. Alternatively, that afternoon we drove out to the visitor center at the Miraflores Locks. In an impressive modern, three-story building, there is a viewing platform where tourists watch the train locomotives, known as *mulas* (or mules), steer ships through one of the locks. Across the canal was a small, white stucco building, covered in red corrugated tiles. It was the original operations and customs house, with the year 1913 inscribed above its doorway.

Inside the museum, a room of computers provides a database with an interactive family history of laborers who worked on the canal. We tried to find Horacio's family, but the program was on the fritz. I spent the next hour looking at photos, old documents and watching a film on the history of the Panama Canal. Cowboy disappeared to somewhere on the viewing platform. The soundproof film room was packed with tourists from around the world. No one moved while the history of the canal was told.

From almost the moment that Vasco Balboa made it across the rugged Darien region of the Isthmus of Panama in 1513 and clapped eyes on the Pacific, building a canal to connect the two oceans became an obsession in Europe, and eventually, America. Balboa hacked out a primitive road across the inhospitable Darien terrain, from Atlantic to Pacific. Little more than a decade after Balboa's discovery, the Holy Roman Emperor, King Charles V, put plans in motion to build a canal; as did the Scots in the 17th century. In 1846, over three centuries after Balboa's discovery, American President James K. Polk signed a treaty with a newly-independent Colombia (of which Panama was a district) that gave the U.S. the right to build a railroad across the isthmus. Like Vanderbilt in Nicaragua, with the California gold rush full on, the inter-oceanic train would transport supplies and people across the isthmus and on to San Francisco.

More than twenty years later, in 1869, the Suez Canal was completed. Riding the glory of that success, French developer Ferdinand

de Lesseps turned his attention to Panama. Preceded by his reputation, Lesseps was granted a concession from Colombia with the
rights to build a canal. He had no trouble attracting French investors.
At the time, sailing around Cape Horn from Le Havre to Vancouver
took forty-four days, but with a "Panama Canal" that trip could be
made in twenty-seven days.

By 1884, thousands of laborers, mostly from the Caribbean
Islands, were building bridges and ports, digging navigational chan-
nels. Over the course of two decades, sixty million cubic meters of
earth were removed, but malaria and smallpox had taken their toll
on the project. Almost 22,000 laborers had perished and investors
felt they were throwing good money after bad. Moreover, the backers
came to realize that building a sea-level, ocean-to-ocean canal was a
different feat in the dry, desert-like conditions of the Suez versus the
disease-infested jungles of Panama. Uncle Sam was chomping at the
bit to take his turn.

In 1903, after Colombia had said no to the U.S. in its sudden
quest to assume control of the canal project, President Theodore
Roosevelt dispatched the battleship U.S.S. *Nashville* to Panama in an
act of gunboat diplomacy, reinforcing the revolutionary junta in
Panama that was, not coincidentally, declaring independence from
Colombia. Fifteen days after the coup and secession, the U.S. and
Panama signed the Hay-Bunau Varilla Treaty, giving "sovereign rights
in perpetuity" to the U.S. French investors were paid forty million
dollars to go away, and Panama became a virtual U.S. colony.

Work on finishing the canal began soon after the treaty signing.
The U.S. Navy controlled the commerce and seas from here to the
Guantanamo naval base, acquired a few years before when Roosevelt
and his Rough Riders played a role in the media-provoked American
intervention in the Spanish-Cuban war. In addition to U.S. public
health doctors controlling the spread of mosquito-borne diseases,
key to the canal's successful completion ten years later was a large

work force (75,000 laborers, 6,000 of whom perished), a narrow isthmus, the mighty Chagres River, an abundance of water, and a well-engineered system of locks and dams that raised Gatun Lake to twenty-five feet above sea level.

On October 10, 1913 President Woodrow Wilson telegraphically signaled the detonation that blew up the Gamboa Dyke: The waters of Gatun Lake flooded the Culebra Cut and the two oceans became one. Three months later, on January 7, 1914, the *Alexandre La Valley*, a vintage French ship, passed through the canal on its own steam. Four centuries after Balboa and his men hacked their way across the Isthmus of Panama and sighted the Pacific Ocean, the sailing distance from New York to San Francisco had been cut from 14,000 to 6,000 miles.

❂ ❂ ❂

Panamanians were never happy with the treaty that gave the U.S. sovereign rights over the Canal Zone. Renegotiated in 1936 and 1955, the modified treaty increased financial payments to Panama and restricted American troops to the Canal Zone. From the Panamanian point of view, these modifications were just band-aids. Through the '50s the nationalist movement and anti-American anger escalated until the '64 riots. After the bloodshed from that unrest was broadcast worldwide, international leaders assailed the American occupation as that of a bullying colonialist, against a backdrop of former European colonies basking in the early days of independence (and as a distant war in Vietnam was escalating).

The forty-five-minute film at the visitor center made use of black and white footage of school boys climbing the Balboa High School flag pole and jumping the "fence of shame" that separated the Canal Zone from the Republic of Panama, amid clouds of tear gas and gun fire. Of the two million tourists who arrive in Panama each year, hundreds of thousands make the trip to Miraflores and watch as I did the historic images of Panama's struggle against U.S. occupation.

⊙ ⊙ ⊙

Two days later Cowboy and I departed Panama, going our separate ways after almost two months on the road. At home in Cambridge, Massachusetts, I began to read my diary and fully absorb our animating journey South. It's fair to say we had captured the beat of a changing world. What came to mind most, however, was the abject poverty, the depth of faith, the environmental degradation, and the unrelenting anti-Americanism we had encountered busing down the Pan American Highway.

For many in Latin America, anti-Americanism is practically an article of faith, if not an acceptable form of prejudice (and has been almost since "American" entered the world's vocabulary). Charles Dickens thought of Americans as ruthless capitalists, like his character Ralph Nickleby, who had no friends other than those who feared him or depended on him for money. Tocqueville talked about "American exceptionalism," a phrase he coined to describe our profound differences with other nations. Our otherness has included being too religious and too proud of our style of democracy, of our individual rights, of our Calvinist sense of election. Our own Herman Melville confirmed this view in his book *White Jacket*: "We Americans are the peculiar, chosen people—the Israel of our time; we bear the ark of the liberties of the world."

An unforeseen outcome of a life of wandering has been to understand the good and bad foreign policy impact Uncle Sam has wrought on other sovereign nations. Beauty is as beauty does. America-bashing is to be expected, given that we are the wealthiest country in the world with the world's most powerful military. On a street level, that means we are the flushest cat on the block, and, if fucked with, we can whip your ass. Hard medicine to swallow for those who are not us. It's even tougher to take when you layer on top of rich-badass, U.S. foreign policy interventions that push weaker nations around because we can.

I've witnessed American-bashing since late adolescence: in the army for twenty-one months in the Vietnam theater of war; among French students protesting the Vietnam War in Paris; watching teenage girls chunking rocks at me in Pakistan over our intervention in Afghanistan; seeing Muslim fundamentalists circling my guesthouse in Khartoum, Sudan, shouting death to America; living in Nairobi, Kenya when al Qaeda blew to smithereens the American Embassy; on a sea journey on a freighter with the German ship captain all but keel-hauling me for being American; in Hanoi a mob of Vietnamese attacking a friend for being American; happening upon demonstrators in South Korea and Guatemala who were protesting Yanks, triggered by a visit by an American President. The list goes on.

An underlying motive or reason always seemed present, sometimes silly as hell or plain old wingnuttery but often deep-seated resentment or anger, and, in more than a few cases, festering like a time bomb. We all have our breaking points. In a nutshell, American-hating is ubiquitous, existential, historical, as is envy or pursuit of the American Dream by the poorest of the poor, along with a shared instinct for self-preservation. Navigating those polarities on foreign soil, tapping into their organic essence, has predictably left this Yankee traveler thinking we are all pieces of the same puzzle, having more in common as humans than what separates us. Treating strangers as I would have them treat me is embedded behavior, as weightless as sunshine.

All those tourists from foreign lands I watched the Panama Canal film with no doubt took away a vivid mental picture of engineering brilliance, and the can-do spirit that has made the U.S. a dynamic superpower. They also remember that: "Yankee Go Home" became a pan-Latin American catchphrase long ago because of the American bullying in Panama. It's all but written in the sky.

183

Epilogue

I'M A WANDERER AT HEART, and as Tolkien reminded us, "not all those who wander are lost." The seeds of a plan, a direction, a continent, riding the rails, an overland route, are always shaking around my noggin, ready to germinate. Advances in communication and modes of travel have shrunken the world to the extent that anything is possible for those on the move. I had hoped to stitch this bus riding journey together with overland trips I've made over the years, and with others on the horizon, and pen a book about the entire 19,000 miles of the Pan American Highway, from the northernmost landfall in the America's, Point Barrow, Alaska, to the southernmost, Tierra del Fuego. Life intervened. That book may still be out there, and if so, it's a couple of years away.

Cowboy and I spent a few days in Belize on this trip, but it felt like a forced detour and I decided to leave it out for several reasons. We didn't explore the country's Maya ruins, or have interesting interactions with locals, and I didn't go scuba diving on the kaleidoscopically diverse Belize Barrier Reef. The underwater adventures in such a complex ecosystem would have been a story unto itself.

El Salvador is the other Central American country missing in this book. As independent travelers, we judged that there were too many political kidnappings, killings, and mutilations going down there to take the risk. Another day awaited.

In late January of 2020, thirteen years after Cowboy and I departed Panama City, my wife Joellen and I landed at Oscar Romero International Airport. To those of us of a certain age and awareness, Oscar Romero was a reminder that El Salvador was, not so long ago, convulsed in a twelve-year civil war. Coffee was king. The "Fair trade" commodity connected El Salvador to the U.S. and beyond with a morning cup of Joe, while dividing the country into a few haves and a few million hole-digging, red berry picking peasants. A zero-sum recipe for unrest.

Romero, the former archbishop of San Salvador, spoke truth to the country's campesinos, urban poor, the military dictatorship, and the "Fourteen Families" of ruling oligarchs who controlled the country's coffee monoculture and wealth. For that he was assassinated by a right-wing death squad in 1980 at a suburban chapel altar while giving communion. The Vatican has since bestowed martyrdom, beatification and sainthood upon Romero.

"History is buried in chain reactions," wrote human rights activist Ayesha Kuwari. "A single event so powerful that it spurs into an unstoppable flurry of trauma that shakes a nation. For El Salvador, that event was the '*La Mantaza*' (The Massacre) of 1932." Up to 40,000 Indigenes and innocent bystanders were slaughtered at the hands of the National Guard and state-sponsored death squads. The fuse was lit, smoldering for decades beneath civility, but fated to burn at a lethal heat. A half a century after La Mantaza, and only months before Romero's assassination, El Salvador erupted volcanically into full on civil war.

By the time the guns of war fell silent and the Chapultepec Peace Accords were signed on January 16, 1992, 80,000 Salvadorans were dead and more than a million either internally displaced or living abroad. Like so many other impoverished and fragilely divided nations, emboldened and financed by foreign proxies to engage in civil wars, no family in El Salvador was left untouched. Everyone has

185

a relative, family friend or acquaintance who fled to Los Angeles, San Jose, Miami, Kansas City, New York, Boston or elsewhere in the U.S. Dollar-denominated remittances from the United States are now El Salvador's largest source of income (twenty-five percent of GDP).

From the jump, every Salvadoran that we had more than a casual conversation with had an upbeat attitude that said it's a new era, anything is possible, including the challenge to attain peace and prosperity. Almost none of El Salvador's grim past or present gang problems were readily apparent to us, or your average tourist, who chilled as we did on the black (volcanic) sand beaches of El Zonte, a world class surfer destination. Our challenges were along the lines of fretting over tidal variations for beach walks, ritually oiling and bronzing the body, reading Joan Didion's "Salvador" and multiple Gabriel Garcia Marquez books, taking in the all-day ballet of surfers catching right-breaking waves, posting up at the Wipe Out Bar for Supremos, Pilsners, and pupusas and watching magical sunsets as pods of pelicans streamed off into the twilight.

After three days of that easy life, restlessness set in. Early one morning, I took off to the west on the C-4 Littoral Highway to the Santa Ana Volcano (7,812 ft.) near the Guatemala border. With a park ranger and two twenty-four-year-old Colombian women joining me, I hiked up the volcano's steep-pitched slopes, furrowed by rows of red ripe coffee cherries ready for harvest. Once we crested, muscles aching, we stared straight down from the vertiginous rim into the turquoise tinted caldera while taking in the panoramic views of the Pacific coast, clusters of extinct volcanoes and a sea of coffee plantations. On the return, the Colombians bounded ahead and I took my time, walking with the ranger. Together, in a stretch of tropical forest, the ranger and I were stopped dead in our tracks, listening with rapt attention to two male bobcats, screeching, snarling, and growling for the affections of a worthy female. It was mating season. Their catcalls were awful and sensuous at once.

186

The following day Joellen and I drove to the populous capital city of San Salvador, the political, financial, and cultural center of the country. Straight away we stumbled onto a rally of vintage American cars. A cherry red '57 Chevy convertible led the way and bringing up the rear was an unmistakable double of the Dukes of Hazzard's General Lee, a 1969 orange Dodge Charger with a rebel flag painted across the rooftop. Humphrey Bogart's 1940 Buick from Casablanca fell in somewhere in the middle of the pack. Americana on full display.

An hour later we were walking through Cuscatlan Park, which had undergone a recent facelift, compliments of a ten-million-dollar angel, Warren Buffett's son, Howard. The park's Monument to Truth and Memory bore a distinct resemblance to the Vietnam Memorial wall in D.C. Otherwise, the woodsy setting of eighteen acres in the heart of San Salvador, struck us as a universal Sunday-in-the-park kind of place with picnickers, manicured playgrounds, lovers on benches, pick up soccer games, skateboarding, a ten-piece salsa band and dancing.

Historic Downtown, crowded with Sunday strollers, throbbed with cumbia and marimba bands. Mimes, magicians and pupusa cart vendors worked the Piccadilly Circus crowds beneath memorials to Columbus and Queen Isabella and the iconic Metropolitan Cathedral with Saint Romero's body entombed beneath. Shades of the past further intruded as heavily armed soldiers/police patrolled the area menacingly wearing black balaclava masks to escape detection by gang members who might be their neighbors in some urban hood. Peace is often a fragile state of mind, definitely no overnight thing.

We spent our last two days in the verdant Sierra Madre winding up and along a patchwork of coffee fields and the colorful Ruta de las Flores and Ruta Artisanal. Along the way was a collage of Indigenous villages, the former FMLN guerrilla hideout of Cinquera, and the Salvadoran cultural Mecca of Suchitoto, in Nahuatl meaning "Place of Flower Birds." These former colonial towns were laid out in the Spanish tradition of a central church as the tallest building facing a tree-shaded, cobblestone plaza and an orderly grid of adobe homes, shops and markets chocked with Indigenous handicrafts. Next to the imposing Santa Lucia Church, as an afternoon pick me up, we sampled a street vendor's soupy *atole*, a sweet Maya beverage of fermented corn served hot.

From Suchitoto's port San Juan we boated to the avian islands of Lake Suchitlan, a major stopover and nesting habitat on the Mesoamerican Flyway, ranging from the Southwest of the United Sates to Colombia. I'm hardly a skilled birder but the sheer volume of winged migrants on and around La Isla de los Pajaros (Island of the Birds) was staggering: white pelicans, neotropic cormorants, great blue herons, whistling ducks, blue-winged teal, and over 200 more species on any given day. On our return to shore the setting sun silhouetted a flock of white pelicans and washed magically over the placid blue waters of Suchitlan and the surrounding Sierra Madre.

❂ ❂ ❂

From El Salvador, we took a short flight to Panama to catch a sailboat that would take us around the San Blas Islands and then across the open sea to Cartagena, Colombia. Many Pan American Highway overlanders are choosing to hop a boat or flight to avoid the Darien Gap, a sixty-mile stretch of inhospitable, outlaw-infested rainforest connecting Central and South America.

From Porto Lindo, on the north Caribbean coast of Panama, on a sixty-four-foot, steel-hulled sailboat named the *Quest*, we joined a hodgepodge of seasoned travelers: Martin, a Canadian cyclist with his bicycle lashed to a bow rail and ready to carry him across Colombia; Sam and Claudia, Kiwis, who'd been on the road in Central America for five months; Danie, a Swiss woman on a year-long peregrination through the Americas; Daniela, an Argentine, working on the boat to fund her travels through Central America and Mexico; Nicole and Justin, a Dutch couple, headed to Patagonia

188

for a few months. All millennial backpackers, and but for Daniela, taking a year or more off from their careers. We were randomly thrown together in close quarters for five days and came out the other side with lasting friendships. Connection, self-discovery, is joy.

Then there was Captain Goeran, a Swede, who took sixteen years to build the Quest with his own hands in a shipyard near Stockholm. He had worked on ships around the world for over three decades, learning to sail and saving money to fund the building of his dream boat. The Quest was his home, his business, his marriage, his life.

I'm told there are only about a dozen assholes in the world, but they sure get around a lot. As we boarded the Quest that day, and handed Captain Goeran our passports, his first words to me and Joellen were: "I hate Americans."

"Well howdy do, here we go again," I replied. "Are all you Swedes alike? Homogenized? Think the same?"

"No, I was married to an American," he snapped back.

"That explains a lot," I hissed, holding back my Sunday punch. "Do us a favor and blame her, not us, for your divorce."

We moved on as he checked other passports. After his introductory surliness, he lightened up. Over the next five days, with all his Nordic candor, we engaged in many conversations about sailing and traveling the world, with more than a little chest bumping.

Captain Goeran ran a tight ship without imposing too many pesky rules. Hands down, my favorite of those was the first: put your sandals in a box in the hold and go barefoot until Cartagena. They say you can't stay forever young, but you can be forever childlike. For four days there was no more friction on the feet than dappled turquoise waters, gleaming white sand beaches, fins for snorkeling or stubbing a toe staggering to the head in the middle of the night. Like all modern-day pirates, our soundtrack was Jimmy Buffett and Bob Marley and our spirit of choice was rum: rum and coke, rum and coconut (Cocoloco), rum out of the bottle, cheap rum, premium rum, more rum.

The San Blas, an indigenous province of the Guna, consists of an archipelago of 365 islands and cays off the north coast of the Isthmus of Panama. Only forty-nine of those islands are inhabited. We saw little of the Guna villages, choosing to sail east and south and anchor each afternoon in the turquoise waters off some uninhabited, idyllic island with powdery white beaches and coconut palm trees. Days were easy to while away, snorkeling with rays, swimming, reading, beach walking, swapping stories, busting open a coconut, and watching a golden tropical sunset and luminous moonrise at the same time.

On our last day in the San Blas, two indigenous (Guna) fishermen, both free divers, delivered twelve freshly caught two-pound lobsters to us from their dugout canoes. That evening as the plumpest of full moons laid a rippled trail of silver right up to the boat, we feasted on the delicacies doused in garlic butter and chased with cheap rum, amid much oohing and ahhing.

Weighing anchor at midnight, the thirty-six-hour open sea sail from the San Blas to Cartagena wasn't for the faint-hearted. Hatches battened, we rolled over ten to fifteen-foot waves, kabooming almost metronomically into a trough every sixth or seventh wave. Nary a sighting of another ship, only flying fish and the occasional frigate bird. But nobody was looking to the sky, most passengers were seasick, nauseated, upchucking. Joellen and I were the only ones who brought along motion sickness patches, so we suffered the least. Daniela relieved Captain Goeran for five-minute catnaps, otherwise he was at the helm the entire thirty-six hours, a committed skipper.

Once anchored in the Cartagena harbor, someone snapped a photo of our diverse group of journeyers. We then dispersed, never to see each other again, into the cobblestone streets of Cartagena's walled Old Town, a UNESCO World Heritage Site and inspiration for the magical realism of Nobel laureate Gabriel Garcia Marquez. Yes, for sure, everything was magical that day.

190

⚙ ⚙ ⚙

Joellen and I did our best to cover large chunks of Colombia in the next three weeks, traveling from Cartagena to Medellin and Bogota and then down the Magdalena River Valley to the pre-Inca archaeological site of San Augustin and the bird-rich Tatacoa Desert.

Across Colombia, street artists have brushed and spray-painted the brick and concrete buildings with punchy graffiti and abstract murals. Each city is an intersection of diverse cultures, using public art as a means for its citizens to define themselves and, almost unconsciously, to stitch together the broader tapestry that is Colombia. Recurring themes often addressed women's rights, anti-racism, anti-imperialism, Indigenous land issues (eighty-seven ethnic groups, sixty-five languages), drug war policies gone amok, guerilla fighters turned activists, and the natural world of snakes and creation myths, cosmic frogs and shamans and jaguar-powerful women. More than once the vibrant colors and swirling images of the public art struck me as a Caribbean way of melding Diego Rivera's murals of the 1930s with Wes Wilson's psychedelic poster art of the 1960s.

From the ochre-tinted canyons of Tatacoa it was onward across the Andes to Ecuador by overnight bus, a thrill-a-minute ride, often careening around hairpins as if a Formula One entrant at Monte Carlo. When the barf bags came out, Joellen did mention that going forward she could do without such cross-cultural experiences. A week later, after traveling south to the Avenue of the Volcanoes and on to Banos, known as the Gateway to the Amazon, we left Ecuador and returned to Cambridge. It was mid-March 2020. The world had turned. The jig was up. The Covid pandemic was upon us.

⚙ ⚙ ⚙

Suddenly I had plenty of time on my hands for reading, pulling up maps, and studying routes. I learned that Will Rogers, a cowboy philosopher and traveling hero, and renowned aviator Wiley Post, died in a plane crash in 1935 near Point Barrow, Alaska. A memorial next to a former Inuit seal camp marks the spot where the single engine Lockheed Orion went down. Paying homage to perhaps two of the world's most famous adventure travelers makes perfect sense as a starting point for the northernmost stretch of the Pan American Highway. Happy trails.

Acknowledgements

OVER THE YEARS random people would ask me the question, "How long have you and Joellen been together?" My tongue-in-cheek reply was that we'd been married twenty-five years, but only been together twelve. That all changed in 2020 with the Covid pandemic. We hunkered down at home, no longer ships passing in the night. Our travel wings were clipped. We are now together 24/7, and our offices are two rooms apart. Almost daily, as I've been working on *Gringos Traveling South of the Rio Grande*, she's made herself available as a sounding board and, at times, full on editor of sentences, paragraphs, pages and chapters. I've said it before: She makes me look better than I am.

Literary friends Mike Boulden, a retired tall building lawyer, and Billy D. Higgins, a Professor Emeritus of History, gave their full attention to reading the manuscript from its earliest iteration, copy editing when necessary, suggesting structural changes and improvements, while always providing encouragement and support. For that, and their stalwart friendship, I am deeply grateful.

The bibliography speaks for itself. I could heap praise one by one on all the books I've included, but I'll keep it brief and only mention *Southern Passage* by Sandy McMath, a fellow Arkansan and distant cousin whom I never met. Had Sandy not passed away in 2025, and I happened to catch his obituary in the *Arkansas-Democrat Gazette*, I would not have known about his entertaining, adventurous and extensively-researched account of traveling from Tijuana to Tierra del Fuego. An invaluable resource, which inevitably improved and deepened this manuscript.

In the end, I vouch for the accuracy of all the details in *Gringos Traveling South of the Rio Grande*.

Phil Karber
Fayetteville, Arkansas
January 28, 2026

Bibliography

Collis, Maurice, *Cortes and Montezuma*, New York, A New Directions Classic, 1999

Forsyth, Susan, *Guatemala*, Victoria, Australia, Lonely Planet, 2004

Finger, Charles J., *Tales from Silver Lands*, New York, Doubleday Page and Company, 1925

Fuller, Alexandria, "Mexico's Pilgrim Cowboys," *National Geographic*, Washington D.C., August 2007

Gorney, Cynthia, "Mexico's Other Border," *National Geographic*, Washington D.C., February 2008

Greene, Graham, *The Power and the Glory*, New York, Penguin Books, 1940

Grillo, Joan, "U.S. Guns Bolster Mexican Traffickers," Miami, *Miami Herald*, August 15, 2007

Hamnett, Brian, *A Concise History of Mexico*, Cambridge, Cambridge University Press, 1999

Herrera, Hayden, Frida, *A Biography of Frida Kahlo*, New York, Perennial, 1984

Huxley, Aldous, *Beyond the Mexique Bay*, New York, Vintage Books, 1960

Johnson, Kevin, "Always on Guard in Nuevo Laredo,"Washington D.C., *USA Today*, May 17, 2006

Katz, Friedrich, *The Life and Times of Pancho Villa*, Stanford, California, Stanford University Press, 1998

Kinzer, Stephen, "Life Under the Ortegas," *The New Yorker*, New York, June 12, 2008

Mann, Charles, *1491, New Revelations of the Americas Before Columbus*, New York, Vintage Books, 2005

Marnham, Patrick, *So Far From God, A Journey to Central America*, New York, Penguin Books, 1985

McMath, Sandy, *Southern Passage, Soundings Overland: Tijuana to Tierra del Fuego*, San Francisco, Discoverer's Press, 1993

Noble, John, *Mexico*, Victoria, Australia, Lonely Planet, 2006

Perera, Victor, *Unfinished Conquest*, Los Angeles, University of California Press, 1993

Perez, Sonia, *Bush, Go Home*, Guatemala City, Guatemala, Prensa Libre, March 12, 2007

Sedgewick, Augustine, *COFFEELAND, One Man's Dark Empire and the Making of Our Favorite Drug*, New York, Penguin Press, 2020

Tobar, Hector, "Guatemala Killings Inquiry Hits Snags," Los Angeles, *Los Angeles Times*, July 6, 2007

Wright, Ronald, *Stolen Continents, 500 Years of Conquest and Resistance in the Americas*, Boston, Houghton Mifflin, 1992

About the Author

PHIL KARBER is a two-time Lowell Thomas Award–winning travel writer. He has journeyed to all continents and 157 of the 193 UN-recognized countries, lived in Africa and Asia for fourteen years, and has authored the following books: *Vagabond Memoirs*; *Postmarks from a Political Traveler*; *Fear and Faith in Paradise: Exploring Conflict and Religion in the Middle East*; *The Indochina Chronicles: Travels in Laos, Cambodia and Vietnam*; and *Yak Pizza to Go: Travels in an Age of Vanishing Cultures and Extinctions*.

www.ingramcontent.com/pod-product-compliance
Lightning Source LLC
Chambersburg PA
CBHW030249130626
46549CB00002B/452